P9-DOA-878

THE TIME TRAP

THE
TIME
TRAP

R. Alec Mackenzie

amacom

A DIVISION OF AMERICAN MANAGEMENT ASSOCIATION

Foreword

It took me twice as long to write this book as I thought it would. The publisher granted me one extension of the manuscript deadline but said that would have to be the last. If it wasn't met, no book.

Well, you know how it goes when you face a deadline; everything goes wrong. Illness strikes and two members of the family are hospitalized without warning. You have to move both your home and your office at the same time. You're beginning a business of your own and find yourself traveling more than half the time.

Funny—or is it?—how time masters all of us. No one seems immune to its ravages. No one has all the answers; only a few seem to have *any*. For the past eight years, I've been seeking them out—these few who seem to have mastered the problems of time, who seem to have all the time they need, who find time enough to do the things they really want to.

I've encountered these exceptional people at seminars and lectures in 10 countries, on planes, in homes of friends.

A Norwegian company president cut his staff meetings in half and began sticking to an agenda. Immediately the participants began to accomplish better results in less time.

The president of a very successful trucking firm in Oklahoma makes very few decisions—only those involving policy considerations. He finds it leaves him time to listen, ask questions, make suggestions, and enjoy his work as well as his leisure.

A Montreal businessman returned from a two-week vacation to the usual stacked desk. By resisting interruptions and focusing his energies on the important matters, he got caught up in three days. He decided that these practices made good sense, so he has kept them up. He has enjoyed all the time he needs for both work and leisure ever since.

An Eastern school superintendent discourages reverse delegation. When someone sends in a problem he thinks should have been handled at a lower level, he returns it with a note asking, "Why are you sending this to me?" Education, he says, is big business today, and the same management principles apply. If he allows himself to get involved in the daily decisions, he won't have time to manage.

A Dutch manager doesn't say yes when his subordinates call to ask if they can come in with a problem. After determining that the problem is not an emergency, he says, "Give me 10 minutes [or whatever time he needs] to complete the task I'm doing. Then I'll come to your office." This saves time, he says, because if he sits down in his own office, the *visitor* is in control. If he goes to the subordinate's office, "I'm in control because I can leave at any time."

Another businessman got tired of a caller who wasted his time on the telephone. One call came at a particularly bad moment. The manager hung up on *himself* in the middle of a sentence. Of course the caller assumed the fault was the phone company's—no one would ever think a person would do that to himself.

You'll meet some of these managers and many others in the pages that follow. Out of hundreds of ideas, the best have been distilled for your consideration.

But charting pathways around major time wasters can be a perilous adventure. At times you will feel that my recommendations have an arbitrary ring. This comes from my conviction that many solutions are self-evident and few of them new. We already know what we should do. We've simply lacked the determination or the self-discipline to do it. So don't be surprised when I come down hard on a point. It may well be one that has had me on the ropes. Though I speak strongly, however, don't feel that I am insisting there is only one way. Time management is a very personal thing. You must select from the dozens of suggestions offered and tailor them to your own needs.

Mastering time is no task for the faint of heart. If you've already succumbed to the slavery of a stacked desk, the tyranny of the telephone, and a relentless stream of interruptions; if you've accepted these conditions as the "executive's way of life"; or if you are looking for an easy way out—for shortcuts in mastering time—then this book is not for you.

If you are among those hardy souls resolved to make the most of the limited time you have, to manage your time more effectively, and if you are willing to pay the price—then read on. Some surprises lie ahead.

R. ALEC MACKENZIE

Chappaqua, New York

Contents

Chapter 1

Time—A Critical
Resource

Do you have enough time? If your answer is a resounding *no,* you are echoing the response of the vast majority of managers.

Of the thousands of managers I have polled, from board chairmen and chief executives to first-line supervisors, only one in a hundred has enough time. When the others have been asked how much more time they would need to do the job they'd like to do, one out of ten says he would need 10 percent more, four say 25 percent, and the remaining half say 50 percent!

This is an alarming, indeed a critical, situation when we realize a startling fact about time—there *isn't* any more of it. Each of us already has all the time there is. Thus we discover the paradox of time: few people have enough; yet everyone has all there is.

As the late Walter Williams, dean of the University of Missouri School of Journalism, told his students, "There's one thing each of you has in exactly the same amount, and that is time." Thus the problem is not time per se. The problem lies within ourselves—the manager, the salesman, the housewife, the professional, the worker. It is not how much we have but rather what we do with the time we have—how well we utilize it.

A Unique Resource

Most of us sense something else about time: it is a resource. Moreover, it is a unique resource. It cannot be accumulated like money or stockpiled like raw materials. We are forced to spend it, whether we choose to or not, and at a fixed rate of 60 seconds every minute. It cannot be turned on and off like a machine or replaced like a man. It is irretrievable. As Chaplin Tyler put it, "Time is the most inexorable and inelastic element in our existence." [1]

We can, however, determine the way we spend it. Like other resources, time is either managed effectively or it is mismanaged. As author and consultant Peter Drucker observed, "Time is the scarcest resource and unless it is managed nothing else can be managed." [2]

Executive time is widely recognized as a critical resource. Analyzing overseas investment decisions, Yair Aharoni has concluded that the most important difference between the experience of some 35 United States companies and the models of decision making is the failure of the models to recognize that executive time is the scarcest resource. [3] John Kitching, examining why corporate mergers succeed or fail, has noted that the lack of appreciation of the new demands on the time of executives in the acquiring company is one of the primary causes of failure. [4]

Curtis Jones proposes that minimization of demands on executive time deserves almost as much attention as businessmen now devote to profit maximization. In fact, "There are many decisions where return on time provides a more useful criterion for action than return on capital invested." [5] The editors of *Business Week* agree with Jones's conviction that time—not money—is a company's most critical resource. "Some companies," they say, "soon may be making capital decisions on the basis of return on the investment of executive time." [6] Moreover, Jones predicts that organizations will begin assigning staff the responsibility of helping executives make the best use of their time.

In management courses, why has the management of time been neglected? Of all resources time appears to be the least understood and the most mismanaged. We seem to have left the ultimate disposal of a priceless commodity unplanned and uncontrolled, subject to the vagaries of chance.

One reason for this oversight may be our failure to recognize that "time management" is actually a misnomer. In the strict sense one does not manage time, for the minute hand is beyond our control. It moves relentlessly on. Time passes at a predetermined rate no matter what we do. It is a question not of managing the clock but of managing ourselves with respect to the clock. Once we see this principle, we readily understand why the management of time brings us face to face with what seems to be a staggering array of problems.

Tagging Time Wasters and Their Causes

We tend to feel that our problems are unique. Yet a striking similarity can be discerned in problems with time at virtually all levels of management in nearly all types of enterprise in every country. Take the matter of time wasters. From Seattle to Heidelberg and from Bogotá to Oslo, I have worked with managers in identifying their major time wasters. They are always similar and often identical. The same thing holds in different kinds of enterprise. For example, 40 colonels and commanders at the Canadian Forces School of Management in Montreal constructed a list of major time wasters virtually identical to one composed by 30 college presidents in the Midwestern United States. Some 300 members of a state association of public school superintendents listed time wasters almost identical to those specified by 25 chief executives of the Young Presidents Organization of Mexico in Mexico City.

A group of salesmen in one of the largest North American insurance companies named nearly the same time wasters as a group of black leaders of religious organizations.

To illustrate this universality, the accompanying list details time wasters of four groups of top managers among those mentioned above. See if you can decide which list belongs to which category: (1) Canadian military officers, (2) black leaders of religious organizations, (3) college presidents, and (4) German managers. After you have attempted to match the lists with the sets of managers, turn to the notes at the end of the book to see the correct correlations.[7]

Two time wasters are omitted that would give away their authorship: "Bosses," which would eliminate the two groups of chief executives, and "Enhancing the democratic process," which would tend to identify the college presidents.

Had we continued the lists, even greater overlap than is already evident would have developed. The omission of "Telephone" by groups C and D does not signify necessarily that the problem does not exist for them. Group C might well have gone on to indicate that "Socializing" includes that done on the phone as well as with drop-in visitors. Group D might have done likewise with "Talking too much."

INTERNAL MONKEY WRENCHES

It is important to note that many time wasters are internally generated. When asked to identify their major time wasters, managers will invariably list external causes first, such as the telephone, meetings, visitors, paperwork, and delays. After time management problems and principles have been discussed, a new source is invariably identified—the man within, generating such time wasters as lack of delegation, fire fighting, lack of plans and priorities, the open-door policy, and procrastination.

This phenomenon can be demonstrated through the use of Peter Drucker's film *Managing Time*. In this film Drucker is visiting with a president who is depicted in the course of a day committing virtually all the major time management sins.

Time Wasters of Four Groups of Top Managers

Group A
Unclear objectives
Poor information
Postponed decisions
Procrastination
Lack of information
Lack of feedback
Routine work
Too much reading
Interruptions
Telephone
No time planning
Meetings
Beautiful secretaries
Lack of competent
  personnel
Lack of delegation
Lack of self-discipline
Visitors
Training new staff
Lack of priorities
Management by crisis

Group B
Scheduled meetings
Unscheduled meetings
Lack of priorities
Failure to delegate
Interruptions
Unavailability of people
Junk mail
Lack of planning
Outside (civic) demands
Poor filing system
Fatigue
Procrastination
Telephone
Questionnaires
Lack of procedure for
  routine matters

Group C
Trash mail
Socializing
Unnecessary meetings
Lack of concentration
Lack of managerial tools
Peer demands on time
Incompetent subordinates
Coffee breaks
Crisis management
Unintelligible
  communications
Procrastination
Lack of clerical staff
Poor physical fitness
Red tape
Pet projects
Lack of priorities

Group D
Attempting too much at
  once
Lack of delegation
Talking too much
Inconsistent actions
No priorities
Span of control
Usurped authority
Can't say no
Lack of planning
Snap decisions
Procrastination
Low morale
Mistakes
Disorganized secretaries
Poor communication
Overoptimism
Responsibility without
  authority

If members of the audience first draft a list of their major time wasters, are shown the film, and then prepare a second list, the second list usually reveals a whole new array of time wasters. When the two lists are compared, it is apparent that the first includes predominantly externally imposed time wasters and the second internally or self-generated factors. To grasp the force of this point, note the two lists of time wasters composed by 40 chief executives of electrical contracting companies. List A was compiled before they saw the Drucker film and list B after they had seen it.

List A	List B
1. Incomplete information presented for solutions to problems	1. Attempting too much at once
2. Employees with problems	2. Unrealistic time estimates
3. Lack of delegation	3. Procrastinating
4. Telephone	4. Lack of organization
5. Routine tasks	5. Failure to listen
6. Lunch	6. Doing it myself
7. Interruptions	7. Unable to say no
8. Meetings	8. Refusal to let others do the job
9. Lack of priorities	9. Delegating responsibility without authority
10. Management by crisis	10. Involving everyone
11. Personal attention to people	11. Bypassing the chain of command
12. Outside activities	12. Snap decisions
13. Poor communication	13. Blaming others
14. Mistakes	14. Personal and outside activities

© R. Alec Mackenzie, 1972.

Isn't it human nature after all to look to others and conditions outside ourselves as the causes of our misfortunes? It takes a painful reassessment, a willingness to be self-critical, to see how much of our ineffectiveness is caused by ourselves. When there is assurance that one can admit error with impunity, the real reasons come to light. As the cartoon character Pogo said: "We has met the enemy and they is us."

SELECT YOUR TIME WASTERS

Now that you have seen the lists of time wasters cited by four separate groups of managers, take several minutes to consider your own. List and rank them on a sheet of paper in order of priority. Do not limit your selection to those shown; use them as thought starters only. Others you may wish to consider might be responding to the urgent rather than the important, a disorganized approach to the job, confused responsibilities, failure to motivate the staff, lack of coordination, waiting for decisions, lack of standards, lack of control points and review procedures, overcontrol, overcommunication, and orientation toward problems rather than opportunities. See page 86 for more time—wasters.

Now ask yourself some questions. Which of your time wasters are generated internally, by *you?* Which are generated externally, by events or by other people? Of those generated externally, which could you control or eliminate? When you have answered these questions thoughtfully, do you agree that in *you* lie both the major causes and the major solutions of your problems with wasted time?

If so, you will doubtless come to the conclusion suggested earlier—that at the heart of time management is management of self. The remaining chapters of this book will outline additional principles and techniques of effective time management that have proved as useful as has pinpointing time wasters. Whether you choose to apply these principles and techniques depends in part on your views of work, time, and leisure, which are interrelated. It also depends on your understanding of some myths of time management.

The Long Executive Day

To crystallize your ideas on work, time, and leisure, let us consider a basic fact of executive life: most executives work very long hours. Surveys indicate that the higher one moves in management, the longer his day and his week. There is a ready rationale for this: more important jobs, heavier responsibilities, more people for whom to be accountable. There is a more obvious rationale, however, to the contrary: promotions up the executive ladder usually bring with them more authority to delegate and of course more people through whom to get the work done.

A Daniel Howard survey shows that the typical executive works a 63-hour week—53 in the office, 10 out. Interestingly, most of the surveyed executives don't consider themselves overworked. Only 34 percent think that they put in too many hours and only 19 percent that they work longer hours than most other executives. Yet despite the length of their workweek, most concede that their key subordinates could run their business without them. The bigger the firm, the more likely that the chairman or the president will say this. Still, a majority (61 percent) of top people in all sizes of firms admit that they are not indispensable. "In view of this admission," says Paul Rice, executive vice-president of Howard Associates, "one may very well wonder why it is necessary [for an executive] to work so hard and to immerse himself in so many of the details of day-to-day operations. He says he needs more time to think and to plan. He should take it." [8]

Herman Krannert, as board chairman of Inland Container Corporation, observed, "When I hear a man talk about how hard he works, and how he hasn't taken a vacation in five years, and how seldom he sees his family I am almost certain that this man will not succeed in the creative aspects of business . . . and . . . most of the important things that have to be done are the result of creative acts." [9]

It is interesting that in our society the syndrome of compulsive overwork and corresponding underleisure seems to be a prevalent affliction. Wayne Oates writes about the "workaholic," who drops out of the human community and is merciless in his demands on himself for peak performance. He is unable to tell the difference between simple loyalty and compulsive overcommitment to his employers or his duties. How does a workaholic know that he is one? Oates suggests that sometimes he finds out only when he suffers a heart attack— or when, as in Oates's case, his five-year-old son asks for an appointment to see him. The syndrome is not confined to men, according to Oates. It can also strike women at home, in offices, in volunteer agencies, and in Women's Lib organizations. Afflicted housewives often overuse the phrase "Let me do it" while complaining of having to clean up after everyone else.[10]

Clarence Randall indicates how to recognize the executive work addict, the self-appointed martyr, the Horatius at the bridge, convinced of his pivotal responsibility, the need for his sacrificial effort, and his monumental contribution to the organization. You will know him by his messy desk (too busy to straighten it out), by papers strewn in disarray (all important papers come to *this* desk), by the hasty sandwich brought in by a harried secretary (too much can go wrong if a man this important is away from his desk too long), by the bulging briefcase lugged out the door after everyone else has gone home (at least *someone* cares enough about the work to worry about it after hours), by the quick kiss for his wife on late arrival home and the impatient query, "Why isn't dinner ready?" (important people mustn't be kept waiting), by that vacation "I haven't taken in 15 years," by the panic departures on emergency trips, and by the inability to meet deadlines—and the endless routine that prevents him from making them.[11]

THE DANGER OF LONG HOURS

Excessive work habits are a bane, not a blessing, to the executive and his company. Says Randall, "Pity the overworked executive! Behind his paperwork ramparts he struggles bravely with a seemingly superhuman load of responsibilities. Burdened with impossible assignments, beset by constant emergencies, he never has a chance to get organized. Pity him—but recognize him for the dangerous liability that he is." [12]

Consider some of the reasons it is detrimental to work such long hours.

Executives who consistently devote more than 45 to 55 hours a week to their jobs are in serious danger of impairing their efficiency. Several studies have established that productivity declines rapidly after eight hours of work. Long hours also encourage executives to adopt the attitude that there is no great press to get something done because "There is always tonight." Thus what could be done in eight hours often stretches out to 10 or 12. This work habit, according to Charles Ford, can spread through an entire organization. [13]

A study by Joseph Trickett of successful and unsuccessful executives indicates that a characteristic of failing executives is their readiness to sacrifice their family lives to their occupational lives. In general a neglect of the family and an overemphasis on the job at the expense of the marriage will eventually lower job performance. [14]

Thus we have a sort of Parkinson's Law in reverse—choosing to extend the time available (whether the task demands it or not), rather than expanding the task to fill the time.

One of industry's responses to the work compulsion is compulsory vacation policies. By prohibiting the accumulation of vacation time, the company supports vacations as essential to re-creation, relaxation, and real respite from the demands of the job.

MYTHS ABOUT HARD WORK

One of the myths of time management is that the harder one works, the more he gets done. Robert Pearse, of Boston University, has labeled this the "buckets-of-sweat syndrome." No direct relationship can be assumed between hard work and positive accomplishment. The adage "Work smarter, not harder" has its root in the recognition of the fallacy of this assumption. In fact, a manager getting little done may well attempt to offset his ineffectiveness by appearing to work hard. Results are seldom, says Pearse, proportional to the buckets of sweat generated. If every hour spent in effective planning saves three to four in execution and insures better results, managers would do well not to permit work to start until it has been carefully thought through. While planning requires time, in the end it saves time and gets better results.

There is another myth with similar implications. It holds that managers who are the most active get the best results. It is not uncommon for insecure workers to perform at activity levels inversely proportional to their certainty of direction and their self-confidence. I well remember early in my career feeling unsure of my objectives and making up for it by vigorous activity. The busier I appeared to be, the more secure I felt. Intense activity frequently acts as a protective reaction against insecurity and growing doubt. A motto in the French cavalry, said a participant in a Paris seminar, is, "When in doubt—gallop!" Americans whistle when afraid of the dark. An observer of the Washington scene described a politician as one who, having lost sight of his objectives, redoubles his efforts. Indeed, care must be exercised to distinguish at all times between activity for its own sake and activity that gets results.

Following a Management Institute for College Presidents, a participant concluded, "Perhaps one of the most significant concepts I gained is that it is not a sin or a poor use of time for an administrator to sit, think, and plan rather than be an activist. That one concept has transformed my whole outlook."

A sales manager I was associated with some years ago believed in economy of effort and planning for desired results. Instead of working late he frequently left early. Once or twice a week, he could be counted on to depart from the office in the middle of the afternoon. When we learned that he left to play golf, a group of us decided to query him at lunch.

If the workloads were so unbalanced that he had a problem keeping busy, a few of us thought we could summon a suggestion or two to help him fill up his time.

He expressed surprise at the questioning and asked what was wrong with finishing work early, as long as it was well done, in order to enjoy some relaxation. When he was hired, he pointed out, he had arranged with the president to leave early on occasion when he was ahead of his schedule and no one was waiting for any information. He asked whether there were any projects in our departments held up on his account or whether he was behind on anything. His questioners reluctantly realized that we were without a case!

This experience has led me often to ask managers when we will have the courage of our convictions and reward results instead of activity. When, for example, will we encourage a man who has accomplished the intended results by noon to absent himself from the office and enjoy the leisure that will permit him to return the following day for another high-performance encounter with demanding tasks? If we want producers of results instead of punchers of time clocks, some day we will have to face the inconsistency of our reward system. As Caroline Bird asks,

> When will we judge work by results achieved instead of time spent? Some people would be happier and more valuable working less than 40 hours a week while others want and need to work more. Schedules would vary from person to person and function to function. . . . Decision-makers not only can make their contribution in fewer hours than computer programmers, for instance, but they need the time "off" to maintain the interests that keep judgment 3-dimensional. . . . Our client-oriented people spend a lot of time out of the office seeing people. Our problem-oriented people often work at home. . . . Only the administrative and service people really need to work in the office from 9 to 5. . . . We don't stop to consider how rare the accident would be that made all of the contributions of all individuals come out to exactly seven hours every day.[15]

If Mrs. Bird's concept were applied, we would be recognizing individual differences both in speed of thinking and in tempo of work.

The time measure overvalues the long job and shakes confidence in the idea or decision that came easily, even though many excellent ones come that way. Few things are good simply because they take time. Many services are valuable in spite of the short time they take. There is no particular reason a report that took two days to prepare is necessarily worth two days of the time of the man who prepared it.

A Philosophy of Time

While the myths of time management help answer the question of why executives work so hard, a more fundamental explanation is that they have an inadequate philosophy of work and leisure. Executives talk of leisure in yearning terms as if it were some dim and distant promised land, very much to be sought after but virtually unattainable. Yet do they really want it? If they do, then why haven't they taken it? Why hasn't the group that has wrung the highest monetary rewards from the economic system—the one group that *could* have more leisure time if it really wanted it—arranged to have it? What begins to seem obvious, though few would admit it openly, is that executives work long hours by choice —a choice based sometimes on fear and sometimes on the inability to use free time constructively.

Along with the compulsions that drive busy executives, then, there seems to be a gnawing uncertainty about what to do with leisure time. They are caught in a bind between the Puritan ethic and the situation ethic. Is it right to loaf? Does this great European pastime, so little known to so many Americans, fit into a philosophy of time? Should leisure be an end in itself, or should it be a means to a higher, nobler end?

Work, Dorothy Sayers proposes, is not the thing one does to live but rather the thing one lives to do.[16] We find here a springboard to the understanding of leisure. When work assumes a worthwhile meaning of its own—when it is what one lives to do and to find fulfillment in—leisure acquires a purposefulness of its own. It becomes a means of self-renewal, of revitalization of our energies and talents for the joyful pursuit of what we are best suited to do.

When job assignments are truly meaningful, the objective is not merely to do the drudgery quickly in order to get to the golf game. Rather it is to allocate tasks in a way that the work can be done with maximum relish and maximum speed. The worker in this arrangement gets pleasure from his job and has time to enjoy his out-of-work activities. One then becomes an extension of the other.

Chapter 2

Managing
Yourself

For 20 years Gerald Achenbach has been the chief executive officer of Piggly Wiggly Southern, one of the most successful chains of supermarkets in the country. He has given considerable thought to the principles of management, the utilization of time, and how the two can fit together to help a manager achieve his life goals as a professional and a whole person. I asked him to summarize his philosophy of managing time. "It's your time you're spending," he said. "You should be its master and not let it master you. You can't master your time unless you're first willing to master yourself."

Unless he manages himself effectively, observes Peter Drucker, no amount of ability, skill, experience, or knowledge will make an executive effective. While most books on management talk about managing the work of others as well as those through whom the work is performed, one can really be certain of managing only himself.[1]

Yet can we "really be certain" of managing ourselves? Have we full command over our own nature? Or would we agree with Walter Judd's assessment of man's predicament, "He is so smart today he controls almost all of nature— except his own nature"? [2]

Appraisal Tools

"Know thyself," said Socrates. Much has been written about appraising one's own skills and talents. The initial popularity of sensitivity training programs may be a reflection of the executive's desire to know more about himself. An evaluation of sensitivity training is beyond the purview of this book. Suffice it to say that it is a powerful tool; it must be handled professionally and with great caution.

Executives sincerely interested in finding out more about themselves have not been content with self-ratings of their own strengths and weaknesses. They have sought anonymous assessments from their staffs and benefited from the comparison of their own ratings with those of others.

Realistic self-appraisal is not easy. The less secure one feels in his position, the less inclined he is to pursue this analysis. But if time management is really managing ourselves with respect to time, a closer look at ourselves is in order, and a number of exploratory instruments have been developed for this purpose.

THE KOSTICK PROFILE

One of the many tools allowing a leader to appraise himself is the Perception and Preference Inventory developed by Max Kostick, professor of psychology, Massachusetts State College at Boston. The personality profile that is drawn from it is used in recruiting, selection, development, and counseling programs in this country and abroad. Perhaps its most interesting application is in assessing team compatibility of individual members.

The profile shown in Exhibit 1 is a composite of two different groups of college presidents.

**Exhibit 1. Profile of college presidents drawn from
Kostick's Perception and Preference Inventory.**

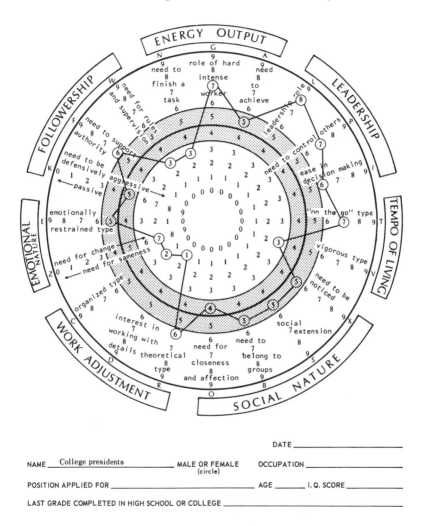

DATE _____

NAME _____College presidents_____ MALE OR FEMALE OCCUPATION _____
(circle)

POSITION APPLIED FOR _____ AGE _____ I.Q. SCORE _____

LAST GRADE COMPLETED IN HIGH SCHOOL OR COLLEGE _____

SOURCE: Max M. Kostick, "Profile for Kostick's Perception and Preference Inventory." Copyright © 1961 by M. M. Kostick, 146 Lancaster Terrace, Brookline, Mass. 02146. Revised May 1963 and September 1971. Reprinted by permission.

TIME STYLES OF LEADERSHIP

Robert Pearse has studied the effect of individual leadership styles on executive skills such as planning, delegating, and decision making. In particular he has evaluated a great number of Kostick profiles and developed the following typical style-related time-use patterns:

1. *Task and achievement orientation* The executive with a strong need to finish tasks personally typically has difficulty delegating. The inner compulsion to finish things makes him feel worthy doing so. Combined with the role of the hard, intense worker, it leads him to pour large amounts of time and energy into doing rather than managing.

2. *Leadership, dominance, and decision orientation* Executives with strong impulses to play the hard-hitting leader role enjoy dominating and controlling subordinates and pride themselves on quick decision making. Theirs is a "take charge" role, and they have difficulty delegating.

3. *Impulsive and physically energetic orientation* These are fast-moving, energetic, action-oriented men who see the executive's job as that of a "shaker and mover." They are often frenetically active, making impulsive decisions and moving back and forth from office to plant with high physical energy.

4. *Socially warm, colorful, and personal orientation* Executives who are high in a need to be noticed enjoy social interaction, like to be emotionally close in interpersonal styles, and tend to spend much of their time in interpersonal relations. Their style contrasts with the task- and achievement-oriented type. They are very successful in positions requiring political relationships, close customer contacts, and the like.

5. *Theoretical, detail, and structure orientation* The theoretical-minded executive is apt to spend much time in careful analysis of abstractions and concepts. He is important in technological companies. He may overlook the practical or implementation part of his work. With a high need to attend to detail personally, he may become a nit picker if not care-

ful. He slows things down by his preoccupation with detail and tends to spend time setting up systems and rigid organization patterns in which he feels most comfortable. He may have emotional difficulty moving freely in unstructured situations.

6. *Change, new-experiences, and feeling-expression orientation*   The change-oriented executive becomes bored with routine. He seeks new experiences and resents work that requires time use in a repetitive pattern. The emotionally calm executive tends to use time in ways that will insulate him from emergencies.

7. *Followership orientation and defensive-aggressive orientation*   The executive who needs to defer to authority spends much time in seeking to please the boss. He is often regarded as "trustworthy." If he does not carry his followership to excess, he may be emotionally soothing to superiors, but he has difficulty managing his own time on independent assignments where he is unable to check with his boss for assurance he is doing what most pleases him. The rules-and-supervision-oriented executive has difficulty structuring his own time unless he has carefully spelled out rules and regulations to go by. He is most comfortable in bureaucratic organizations where he may carry out assignments by the book. The defensive-aggressive executive carries a large chip on his shoulder and spends time arguing with others. He may feel others are out to get him. He loves a good fight and so attacks or counterattacks either in one-to-one business relationships or on teams or committees.

Pearse recommends training executives in the skill of time utilization in order to improve their handling of paperwork, delegation, supervision, and planning. Awareness of personal styles may be helpful to the executive rating high in personal attention to detail, an orientation that can be modified with intelligent practice. The impulsive, physically active, and energetic wheel spinner can learn to analyze objectively the waste motion that usually accompanies his fast-paced shaker-and-mover style.[3]

Among the many other recent authors writing on styles of

leadership, Glenn Bassett draws a very interesting comparison between short-term and long-range time management styles:

Time is an often overlooked resource. It is often overlooked because the two fundamental polarities of managerial style tend to trap people into one or another of two time orientations: the realistic style of managing emphasizes the short term, the immediate, the here and now, and it severely downgrades the future as a problem-solving resource. The idealistic style, on the other hand, tends to treat time in much the same way that other resources are treated. It is something to spend and use to one's own purposes. The manner in which the resource of time is utilized is related to and typically limited by the existence of tendencies toward either a realistic or idealistic style of managing. Too often, the fullest use of the resource of time is not achieved because of a realistic orientation, or, conversely, the idealist fails to recognize time constraints which, if not met, could destroy the effectiveness of all other efforts.[4]

The Time Log

From the earliest efforts to log their time, executives have found that their time allotments were not going where they thought they were. Sune Carlson commented after his study of Swedish managing directors, "It is quite a different thing for an executive to *feel* he does not have enough time to work alone or to discuss questions of development with his subordinates, and to *know* how much time he spent alone in his office during the last month, or how many times development questions actually were discussed during the same period."[5]

Peter Drucker's remarks about the time log are enlightening. He observes that approaches to getting more work done always begin with planning. However, effective executives do not start this way. They know that if you start with a plan, it ends up in the bottom drawer. Other plans will follow, winding up in the same place. Instead, according to Drucker, the astute executive begins by finding out where his time is really going.

The time inventory, or log, is necessary because the painful task of changing our habits requires far more conviction than we can build from learning about the experience of others. We need the amazing revelation of the great portions of time we are wasting to provide the determination to manage ourselves more effectively in this respect.

The four lists of time wasters given on page 5 should be proof of one thing—we think our time wasters are primarily external forces until we see a picture of ourselves. The honest time log will give us that picture. We will find a number of unsuspected enemies of time. One surprise will be that time is generally wasted in the same way every day.

Gerald Achenbach found the time log necessary because of a tendency to neglect priorities. He schedules an occasional test on himself for a few days to check this tendency.

In the Sune Carlson study, none of the managing directors, with one exception, was able to work more than 20 minutes at a time on one project. The exception worked at home for an hour and a half each morning. Most of them had 34 to 40 different things to do during a typical day, each lasting from 3 to 20 minutes. None had an uninterrupted period in which to reflect upon the philosophy of management and the policies of the firm. None had a long-range plan for his own work. Their appointment calendars were filled in accordance not with the necessities of the firm but rather with the will of the most energetic or bothersome person. Carlson's conclusion: "Up to now I imagined the boss as a bandmaster leading an orchestra. Now I know that this comparison is wrong, and I rather imagine the boss as a puppet whose strings are drawn by a crowd of unknown and unorganized people." [6]

The Carlson profiles reveal many miscalculations in the executives' minds concerning where their time went. They were mistaken about the amount of inspection accomplished, though they all placed personal inspection tours of plants and offices as among their most important duties. Many estimated they inspected "once a fortnight" or every three weeks, when they hadn't actually done so in several months. They knew of course that they hadn't made the tour the previous month, but there was a special reason for it; not the month before either, but that was also because of something extraordinary. They had forgotten, in fact, how very long it had been since their intention to make an inspection had been carried out.

Managers in a *Fortune* 500 company recently logged their time for several days. Most of them protested that they were not inventorying a "typical" week. It did not seem to occur to them that there *was* no "typical" week and that they should plan for the atypical.

Time logs provide still another surprise—the small fraction of the day that is free or uncommitted. When executives recognize that they have only one and a half or two hours of "discretionary time" at best, says Drucker, they realize that this indeed is their scarcest resource. Concentrating on time wasters, they are often able to extend this discretionary time by having visitors and calls screened and arranging to return calls at a designated hour.

The time inventory is most valuable to the chief executive, who alone is judge of his own performance. The task of self-observation is difficult, as I have said, but the time log is a useful tool to accomplish this objective.

EXECUTIVE TIME INVENTORIES

The executive time inventory shown in Exhibit 2 was developed with three distinct purposes in mind: (1) to require the planned allocation of the executive's time, (2) to require a daily listing of the most important tasks to be accomplished on the following day, (3) to require a daily estimate of effectiveness, based on the number of priority tasks that were actually completed and on the proportional utilization of time as measured against its planned allocation. Following are specific instructions for use of the inventory.

1. Allocate time Decide on principle categories of time expended and the percentage of your time you wish to allocate to each. Such categories might include "board," "team," "dictation," "fund raising," "meetings," and, of course, "wasted." Use specific categories, avoiding vague words like "thinking." Place the categories and the proposed percentage allocations in the columns under "Allocation."

Exhibit 2. An executive time inventory.

	MON. 1. 2. 3. 4. 5.	CATEGORY #	TUES. 1. 2. 3. 4. 5.	CATEGORY #	WED. 1. 2. 3. 4. 5.	CATEGORY #	THURS. 1. 2. 3. 4. 5.	CATEGORY #	FRI. 1. 2. 3. 4. 5.	CATEGORY #	SAT. 1. 2. 3. 4. 5.	CATEGORY #	
Daily Goals													
9:00													
9:30													
10:00													
10:30													
11:00													
11:30													
3:00													
3:30													
4:00													
4:30													
5:00													

ALLOCATION Category | %	Time Spent	% of Day	Time Spent	% of Day	Time Spent	% of Day	Time Spent	% of Day	Time Spent	% of Day	Time Spent	% of Day	SUMMARY Total Time Spent | % of Week
1.													
2.													
3.													
4.													
5.													
6.													
7.													
8.													
Estimate of Effectiveness													

SOURCE: Adapted from R. Alec Mackenzie, *Managing Time at the Top* (New York: The Presidents Association, 1970). Copyright © 1970 by The Presidents Association.

2. *Set daily goals*   Each afternoon before leaving work, list the principle items to be accomplished the following day (set objectives) and arrange them in order of importance (order priorities). Write these at the top of the page in the indicated space, taking particular note of the priority of each.

3. *Keep record of time*   As the day progresses, record results achieved for every 15-minute period. *Do not* wait until the end of the day to fill in the chart. Memory is deceptive, and you will be deceiving yourself. For brevity you may wish to use numerals to represent the broad categories you listed. (Small boxes are provided for this purpose.) For example, if your third category were dictation and at 9:30 you dictated two letters, one to Smith and one to Jones, you might simply enter "Smith/Jones" in the large box and "3" in the small box.

4. *Summarize for a week or more*   After you have kept the inventory for at least one week (two typical weeks are recommended), add the total hours spent in each category and place the totals in the far right-hand column by category. Then compute the percentage of the total time spent on each category.

5. *Estimate daily effectiveness*   On the basis of "Daily Goals" accomplished and how well your time actually spent compared with your planned allocation, estimate your effectiveness for each day. If it exceeds 30 percent, you are above the estimated national "average."

6. *Evaluate*   On the basis of your own objectives for a time management program (such as setting daily objectives and priorities; avoiding interruptions; completing tasks before starting new ones; and so on), analyze your areas of greatest effectiveness and those of least effectiveness. Plan a strategy for improvement. Implement this strategy immediately.

Most managers find, after using this inventory for two weeks, that a great deal of their work is repetitive and should be routinized and delegated. There are many conversations with the same people on the same or similar subjects. There are many phone calls and visits—some important, others not. Thinking and planning seem to be fitted in only if there is time left over.

Many managers use an inventory to set themselves deadlines. Suppose that "Board agenda" is the top priority for Tuesday, designated by the number 1. By placing this item at 10:00 A.M. on the inventory for the day, the executive sets his target of completing this No. 1 priority by 10:00 A.M. Such self-imposed deadlines are one of the most effective techniques of insuring productive effort by monitoring progress. Wrist alarms serve a similar purpose. These devices are useful in initiating new habits.

In reviewing the daily activities, the executive can easily see who has taken the initiative in conversations, meetings, and phone calls, and whether time for planning and thinking is really systematically reserved or is only taken from the residue after other activities have been fulfilled. Were these different contacts designed for obtaining information for himself or others or for decision making?

A daily time analysis, which permits a more detailed recording and diagnosis of activity, is shown in Exhibit 3. Beside it are instructions for its use and questions to be answered immediately following completion of the daily time log.

The problem confronts executives of how long a time segment to log. Because of the cyclical nature of many major tasks, such as planning, a work day in January may be quite different in nature from one in July. Any number of emergency developments in any of the operational areas may involve executives and create radically untypical days. Saxon Tate, managing director of Canada and Dominion Sugar, in Montreal, feels it would be necessary to continue an inventory for an entire year to catch all the variations and be really accurate. Most consultants suggest one or two weeks. Managers at General Foods Corporation take a two-day log before a seminar session on time management. This exercise has the advantage of being relatively easy to prepare while still providing very useful insights into their time utilization, according to JoAnn Weichert, associate manager for development programs. Following the two-day time log, managers are asked to answer questions such as those listed in Exhibit 3.

Exhibit 3. A daily time analysis.

| Goals: 1. _____ 4. _____ |
| 2. _____ 5. _____ |
| 3. _____ 6. _____ |

Date: _____

Time	Action	Priority	Comment, Disposition, or Results
		1 = Important and urgent 2 = Important, not urgent 3 = Urgent, not important 4 = Routine	Delegate to _____. Train _____ to handle. Next time ask his recommendation. Consolidate, eliminate, or cut time. Other.
8:00			
8:30			
9:00			
9:30			
10:00			
10:30			
2:00			
2:30			
3:00			
3:30			
4:00			
4:30			
5:00			
5:30			
Evening			

© R. Alec Mackenzie, 1972.

Instructions for the Daily Time Analysis

1. Enter the date and list the goals for the day in terms of results, not activities. (For example, a goal should read: "Complete agenda within time allocated for sales meeting," not "hold" sales meeting.")
2. Record all significant activities in terms of results during each 15-minute period. Do not wait until noon or the end of the day. The major benefit is lost.
3. Answer the following questions immediately after the completion of the daily time log.

Questions

1. Did setting daily goals and times for completion improve my effectiveness? If so, why? If not, why not?
2. What was the longest period of time without interruption?
3. In order of importance, which interruptions were most costly?
4. What can be done to eliminate or control them?
   a. Which telephone calls were unnecessary?
   b. Which telephone calls could have been shorter or more effective?
   c. Which visits were unnecessary?
   d. Which visits could have been shorter or more effective?
5. How much time was spent in meetings?
   a. How much was necessary?
   b. How could more have been accomplished in less time?
6. Did I tend to record "activities" or "results"?
7. How many of my daily goals contributed directly to my long-range objectives?
8. Did a "self-correcting" tendency appear as I recorded my actions?
9. What two or three steps could I now take to improve my effectiveness?

© R. Alec Mackenzie, 1972.

Birger Wist, president of Bjarne Wist, in Trondheim, Nor-
way, decided on a two-month period for his time log. He kept
a detailed account with the help of his secretary and carefully analyzed the results, which appear in Table 1. The column titled "Forecast" shows the percentage of total time that
he thought he was giving to each function. The column
headed "Actual" indicates the percentage of time actually
spent in each activity.

Table 1   Time Profile of a President

Activity	Forecast	Actual	Planned
1. Planning	50%	30%	40%
2. Reports and control	20	10	5
3. Staff meetings	15	21	10
4. Secretary	5	3	5
Dictation			5
5. Telephone	5	8	5
6. Civic activities	5	20	25
7. Plant visits	0	8	5
	100%	100%	100%

© R. Alec Mackenzie, 1972.

Wist's average working week totaled 35 hours plus time
spent reading management literature. The greatest surprises
to him (not his secretary) were the amounts of time spent on
civic affairs and meetings and his overestimate of planning
time by 20 percent.

As a result of Wist's survey of his use of time, he now plans
(see the third column of Table 1) to spend 40 percent of his
time planning and 5 percent on reports and control. The latter
seemed to be taking longer than desired because of the number of reports he was reading unnecessarily and the number
of questions he would ask that might have been answered in
the reports if the information had been requested. He plans
to reduce this time to 5 percent of his total by delegating the
handling of many reports to others.

Staff meetings, Wist discovered, took much more time than

desired. Better planning, careful preparation of agendas, stronger leadership, and better listening have cut this time in half and have resulted in faster decisions and more progress. Impromptu meetings, often held standing up to discourage socializing, are called frequently for short discussions and fast decisions.

His secretary handles all calls by responding that he is busy and will return the call later, unless of course it is a real emergency. Wist finds this prevents the telephone from running him and allows him to return calls at a time convenient for him. Also he is better prepared to respond since his secretary will know the purpose of the call and provide him with any necessary information.

Plant visits are better planned, and many questions are prepared in advance so that each visit has a definite purpose. Most interestingly, Wist decided that civic responsibilities ought to play an even more important part in his time allocation and he has raised the apportionment to 25 percent.

"I lived with many time wasters for years," says Wist, "but I finally realized that I must do something about them if my business and I were to survive. Even now I find myself gradually slipping back into the old bad habits. So I've decided that I'll repeat the inventory at least briefly as a spot check twice a year."

TIME PROFILES OF EXECUTIVES AND THEIR TEAMS

The ideal allocation of a top manager's time is a matter about which there has been much conjecture but little definitive study. A useful model is shown in the time profile of a company president and his team shown in Exhibit 4. Circles are used to designate the total time of the president and each team member. The inner part of the president's circle, in the center, shows a suggested allocation of the chief executive's time to the managerial functions of planning, organizing, and so forth. The outer band indicates the relative time he devotes to the members of his team. Because this will vary with the nature of the business, the style of the leader, and the

Exhibit 4. A time profile of a company president and his team.

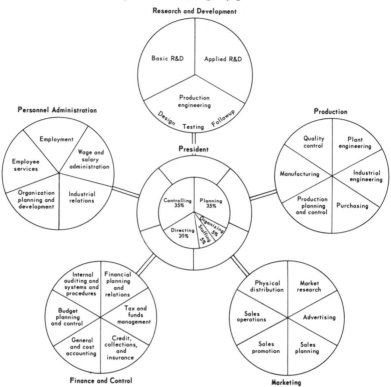

© R. Alec Mackenzie, 1972.

needs of his group, the allocation shown provides for equal amounts of time for each.

Each of the outer circles represents one of the members of the top team with equal divisions among the principal activities of the particular operational function. Thus the vice-president for production is shown responsible for the activities of production planning and control, manufacturing, quality control, plant engineering, industrial engineering, and purchasing. His time allocation to each of these will depend on the nature of the business, the product mix, special organization problems, and the capabilities of his particular team.

The results of a survey of six college presidents and their teams are shown in Exhibit 5. The profile illustrates the striking impact of the current financial plight of most small private colleges on their presidents' time allocation. These administrators agreed that approximately 70 percent of their time at present must be devoted to development and external affairs primarily associated with fund raising.

Exhibit 5. A time profile of six college presidents and their teams.

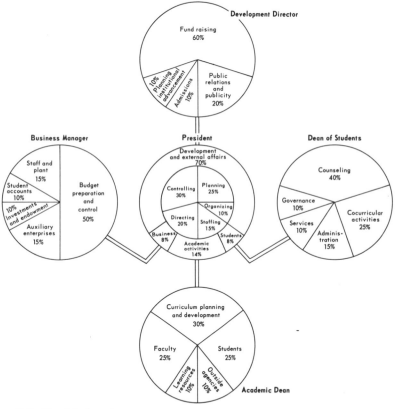

© R. Alec Mackenzie, 1972.

The outer circles, representing the time allocations of chief staff members, were derived by averaging their individual estimates and those of their presidents. A few differences emerged in comparisons of these estimates. For example, the development directors felt they should be allocating more time to planning institutional advancement than did their presidents. The reverse was true of the relative times proposed for fund raising.

The college administrators engaging in this exercise felt that it brought a number of interesting views to light and provided a useful model against which to measure their actual time expenditures.

A Matter of Habit

All self-management involves habits, and removing internally generated time wasters requires changing habits. In dealing with the task of changing behavior and breaking habits, William James, the noted student of the human mind, provided considerable insight:

> "Habit a second nature? Habit is ten times nature," the Duke of Wellington exclaimed; and the degree to which this is true no one can appreciate as well as a veteran soldier. Daily drill and years of discipline make a man over in most of his conduct.
>
> Habit is the flywheel of society, its most precious conserving agent. The great thing, then, is to make our nervous system our ally instead of our enemy. We must make automatic and habitual, as early as possible, as many useful actions as we can, and guard against growing into ways that are disadvantageous as we guard against the plague. The more of the details of our daily life we can hand over to the effortless custody of automatism, the more our higher powers of mind will be set free for their proper work. There is no more miserable person than one in whom nothing is habitual but indecision, and for whom the lighting of every cigar, the drinking of every cup, the time of rising and going to bed every day, and the beginning of every bit of work, are subjects of deliberation. Half the time of such a man goes to deciding or regretting matters which ought to be so ingrained in him as practically not to exist for his consciousness at all.[7]

Karl Menninger, the distinguished psychiatrist and author, said in commenting on James's views:

Over 75 years ago the great American psychologist William James wrote a scientific treatise on what until then had generally been thought of as a moral problem: how to develop good habits and how to break bad ones. This was almost the first application of science to problems of human behavior, and the essay is as sound today as when it was written.[8]

James points to three great keys to the acquisition of new habits and the breaking off of old ones.

1. *Launch the new practice as strongly as possible* Set up a routine that contrasts with the old way. Announce the change publicly, if you can. In short, surround your resolution with every aid you know. This gives you momentum so that the temptation to backslide will not occur so soon as it might, and every day a breakdown is postponed adds to the chances that the new practice will survive.

2. *Never let an exception occur until the new habit is firmly rooted* A lapse is like a skid in a car. It takes a good deal more effort to recover control than to maintain it from the outset. A slip can damp the energy of all future attempts. Acquiring the new habit quickly is the best way if there is to be a real possibility of instilling it. Be careful not to take on such a stiff task as to insure its defeat at the outset. But provided you can stand it, a short period of hard effort followed by freedom from hankering is best to aim at, whether in giving up a habit like drinking or simply changing the hour you get up in the morning. It is surprising how soon a desire will die if it is *never* fed.

3. *Seize the first possible chance to act on your resolution* Resolutions communicate a new "set" to the brain not when they are formed but when they produce motor effects. You may have resolved many times to work on remembering people's names better. Yet until you actually use a person's name in conversation, the process of etching it in your memory will not have begun. As James put it, "A tendency to act becomes effectively ingrained in us only in proportion to the frequency with which the actions actually occur. When a resolve or a fine glow of feeling is allowed to evaporate without bearing practical fruit, it is worse than a chance lost; it

works so as positively to hinder the discharge of future resolutions and emotions. . . ." [9]

If we realized the extent to which we are mere walking bundles of habits, we would give more heed to their formation. We are spinning our own fates, good or evil, difficult to be undone. James cites the drunken Rip Van Winkle in Joseph Jefferson's play who excuses himself for every fresh dereliction by saying, "I won't count this time!" Well, he and kind heaven may not count it, but it is being counted nonetheless. Down among his nerve cells, the molecules are counting it, storing it up to be used against him when the next temptation comes.

We should be careful, of course, to distinguish between good habits and bad. Auren Uris describes the former as adaptive habits—for example, checking the mail first in the morning because it contains orders that influence the day's sequence of business. Nonadaptive habits he describes as illogical and time-wasting—going through the mail each morning as a routine if only ordinary matters are to be discovered which, when handled later, will require a review of the material already read. Thus a useful habit with a clear purpose may outlive its usefulness and become a waste of time. Other nonadaptive habits include interfering with work after you have delegated it, saying yes to outside invitations when you ought to say no, and welcoming every drop-in visitor who wants to spend some time with you because he really has nothing better to do at the moment.[10]

GETTING STARTED

Does the following routine sound at all familiar? Joe has been asked to check some personnel forms. As he starts the job, however, someone phones to ask about an overdue inventory report. So he gets out the inventory file but stops to take a glance at the mail at the same time. A letter on the top complaining about something in the machine shop catches his eye. He drops the inventory file, reads the letter, then starts for the machine shop to discuss it. On the way he passes the cafeteria and the coffee smells so good he decides to interrupt his busy morning and have a cup. His day's accomplishments so far: exactly nothing.[11]

He has failed, it seems, to get started.

Many difficulties confront us in getting off and running. Joe appears to be drifting from one cue to another in a random fashion. The matters he is allowing to distract him do not warrant the interruption. Halfway through the morning, he has not completed the first task he took up. He has, however, drunk his coffee. If we judge what is important to people by what they do with their time, then we must conclude that Joe's priorities are in sad disarray. The aroma from a cup of coffee has taken precedence over everything else he has encountered. It is the only thing from which he has not gotten distracted.

PROCRASTINATING

Often an unpleasant task will be avoided deliberately. Procrastination ranks high on the list of time wasters of nearly every group of managers. It is a close relative of incompetence and a handmaiden of inefficiency. Managers who habitually procrastinate become interruption-prone and actually invite interruptions. The welcome mat is always out for a diversion. Thus a host of time wasters—visitors, meetings, phone calls—invade the executive's domain.

The demands on the manager to manage himself are unending. Time slippage occurs in not getting started, discussions, disorganization, paperwork, overinvolvement, minutiae, and office trivia.

Countering these habits requires self-discipline and perseverance. Norman Vincent Peale describes how procrastination nearly swamped him until he faced up to it. These simple guidelines won his battle:

1. *Pick one area where procrastination plagues you— and conquer it* Peale used to delay refusing speaking engagements he couldn't accept because he didn't like to turn people down. Often he delayed until he couldn't back out. When he began making decisions quickly, he was happier, and so were the people he was dealing with.

2. *Learn to set priorities and focus on one problem at a time* Peale recalled an information desk clerk in Grand

Central Station who was constantly beset by crowds of clamoring, demanding people. However, the man never became flustered. Picking out one of the throng, he would ask the person what his problem was, answer the question slowly and distinctly, and not shift his attention until the person was satisfied. Then he would fix his gaze deliberately on another and proceed. When his turn came, Peale complimented the clerk on his poise and concentration. The man smiled and said, "I've learned to focus on one person at a time and to stick with his problem until it's settled. Otherwise I'd go mad."

3. *Give yourself deadlines* Set deadlines for yourself and let them be known. Ask a friend to check up on you.

4. *Don't duck the most difficult problems* That just insures the hardest part will be left when you're most tired. Get the big one done—it's downhill from then on.

5. *Don't let perfectionism paralyze you* If you put everything off till you're sure of it, you'll get nothing done.[12]

SINGLE HANDLING AND FOLLOWING THROUGH

There are two vital habits in dealing with self-management that are important to mention. The first is the habit of single handling: making a decision, disposing of a letter or report, or taking the indicated action the first time the opportunity presents itself. Normally this is when the document is first picked up from the in basket. This habit requires practice and an iron will. Papers that cannot be dealt with because of insufficient information should be sent to subordinates, to the appropriate person for fact gathering, or to the secretary for her follow-up file until the information is available.

Charles Flory, a partner in Rohrer, Hibler and Replogle, points out that the "do it now" executive is rare. Flory listed this manager at the top of his list of effective executives, with good reason.

The second vital habit is that of doing one thing at a time —and finishing it. Don't lose valuable hours by skipping from one job to another. Complete the one you are on even if it means working through part of your lunch hour. Finishing a task in one session represents a great saving of time because you need not reorient yourself to the facts of the situation and pick up lost threads as you would at a second sitting.

John Mee, of Indiana University, calls this "compulsion to closure": the quality that forces a manager to complete the task. The motivation is the sense of accomplishment that one feels when the intended objective is achieved.[13]

Early in this century, Orison Marden wrote a book about managers who never formed the habits of accuracy, thoroughness, and doing things to a finish. His fascinating work calls men who complete what they undertake, who leave nothing half-done, "a blessing to civilization." "Make it a life-rule," the author pleads, "to give your best to whatever passes through your hands."[14] In a similar vein, the "doctrine of completed staff work," says Louis Allen, holds that the manager who can delegate to the men under him the responsibility for doing a "whole job" is helping himself as well as his organization.[15]

In reviewing candidates' qualifications for top executive positions, executive search firms take particular interest in what a man's record says about projects initiated and carried out. "How is he on followthrough?" is a critical question. It relates not only to the probability that the man can be depended on to conclude a project but more importantly to the certainty that time already invested in the project will not be wasted.

The ability to concentrate—to persevere on a course without distraction or diversion—is a power that has enabled men of moderate capabilities to reach heights of attainment that have eluded the genius. They have no secret formula other than to persevere. Such men must have learned their limitations early, and they must have learned also that concentrated effort over a protracted period can be more productive than a momentary flash of genius. They are unlikely to succumb to that hidden but insidious time waster, the habit of leaving tasks unfinished.

Chapter 3

Planning

Your Work

Nothing is easier than being busy and nothing more difficult than being effective. The hardest managerial work is thinking, an activity too often neglected by managers. Bernard Baruch said once, "Whatever failures I have known, whatever errors I have committed, whatever follies I have witnessed in private and public life, have been the consequence of action without thought." [1]

The utility of planning the day's work is seen clearly in a well-known story concerning Charles Schwab. When he was president of Bethlehem Steel, he presented Ivy Lee, a consultant, with an unusual challenge. "Show me a way to get more things done with my time," he said, "and I'll pay you any fee within reason."

Handing Schwab a sheet of paper, Lee said, "Write down the most important tasks you have to do tomorrow and number them in order of importance. When you arrive in the morning, begin at once on No. 1 and stay on it till it's completed. Recheck your priorities; then begin with No. 2. If any task takes all day, never mind. Stick with it as long as it's the most important one. If you don't finish them all, you probably couldn't do so with any other method, and without some system you'd probably not even decide which one was most important. Make this a habit every working day. When it works for you, give it to your men. Try it as long as you like. Then send me your check for what you think it's worth."

Some weeks later Schwab sent Lee a check for $25,000 with a note saying that the lesson was the most profitable he had ever learned. In five years this plan was largely responsible for turning Bethlehem Steel Corporation into the biggest independent steel producer in the world. And it helped make Charles Schwab $100 million and the best-known steel man in the world. Schwab's friends asked him later about the payment of so high a fee for such a simple idea. Schwab responded by asking, what ideas are not basically simple? He reminded them that for the first time not only he but his entire team were getting first things done first. On reflection Schwab allowed that perhaps the expenditure was the most valuable investment Bethlehem Steel had made all year.[2]

In a very real sense, planning is where it all begins in management. It is the rational predetermination of where you want to go and how you intend to get there. Until this has been done, there can be no assurance that effort expended will be in the right direction. As the Roman philosopher Seneca advised, "When a man does not know what harbor he is heading for, no wind is the right one." There are a few men who make a rewarding port by accepting any wind that is blowing. But recognizing man's willingness to assume credit for happy though unplanned endings, David Jaquith, president of Vega Industries, observed, "Good results without good planning come from good luck, not good management."

Why We Don't Plan Ahead

Human nature appears to work against our planning—even for the day ahead. We seem to feel that predetermining our course of action limits our freedom. Most of us prize this freedom and resist conforming to set patterns. Many managers are natural leaders who make judgments by intuition without conscious forethought. For the great majority, however, as work expands and grows more complex, planning becomes imperative to visualize not only what it is we want to happen but also the various alternatives for accomplishing it.

Yet barriers to planning are numerous. Emphasis on day-to-day operations almost always pushes planning into the background. Putting out today's fires takes priority over planning for tomorrow. Ironically, fire fighting interferes with fire prevention. Uncertainty about the future is also a deterrent to planning. Winston Churchill made this point well when he observed that it is difficult to look farther ahead than you can see. Most of us feel more comfortable working within a structured situation where factors are certain and predictable. Yet the higher one moves in management, the less structured is his job and the further in the future are his goals. Lecturer William Oncken describes this zone of less structured activity as the "area of ambiguity," and a manager's tolerance for it will determine his effectiveness to a great extent.

The principal reasons managers resist planning are summarized by Jaquith as the time, thought, paperwork, procedures, and commitment it entails.

The president of a fast-growing group of companies in Mexico City described the reactions of his men to their initial encounter with the planning process. It seemed so time-consuming to them that they all wished they could forget it and get back to work. They were uniformly discouraged when the requirements in time invested seemed out of all proportion to any immediately identifiable gains. The lack of immediate satisfaction from on-the-spot action overshadowed the prospect of eventual gratification as a result of effective long-range planning.

The urgency of tasks at hand usually takes priority. A humorous line in current vogue speaks to this point: "We all know about the importance of setting objectives, but when you're up to your neck in alligators, it doesn't help much to be reminded that your objective was to drain the swamp!" The deeper the mess, the more intimidating the pile on the desk, then the less excited the manager is apt to be about taking time to plan. Yet in the long run it's his only hope. For every manager who has succumbed to the pull of the immediate, there are others who have fought the battle through and who have come to recognize that survival depends on effective planning. Top management executives of Bray Lines, a very successful trucking firm in Oklahoma, initially reacted unfavorably to the time taken up by a new planning process. Now that the results are clear, they defend it as profitable and essential—and a key factor in the company's outstanding growth record during the recession of 1970–1971.

The avalanche of paperwork that has engulfed the manager's desk has led to an understandable aversion to additional burdens. If developed carelessly or without due regard for economy of effort, the paperwork of the planning program can bury both the planners and those who carry out the plan. Procedures may become complex and onerous. Emphasis ought to be on simplicity, economy of effort, and results.

In the final analysis a plan agreed to means commitment on the part of those agreeing. Managers involved in the planning process recognize that the ultimate choice of a course of action involves commitment to the achievement of stated objectives.

PLANNING TIME SAVES TIME

Managers who resist planning because they "don't have time" are failing to look ahead to the significant long-range savings in time as well as the improved performance that usually results. Crawford Greenewalt, former president of Du Pont, observed that the top-notch workers are those who first plan and then follow a relaxed rather than a frantic pace. "Planning their time makes this ease possible," said Greenewalt, "for every moment spent planning saves three or four in execution." [3]

Investing time to save time is not the easiest concept to get across, as the president of a Midwestern manufacturing company discovered when he undertook to sell the idea to his top team members. They demurred. Take time out of their already heavy schedules to plan? They could readily visualize other projects with more obvious and immediate benefits. "When you are swamped with more to do than you can get done," they asked, "how do you find time to plan?"

A good question. It required an answer. Company projects of a repetitive nature that were subject to measurement were selected, and a careful record was kept of the planning versus the execution time of each. On a second group of projects similar to the first, the planning time was extended. These were executed significantly more quickly, saving considerable time overall (see Exhibit 6). In addition, the executives found the projects netted better results. Clearly, sound management in the area of planning *can* help managers to get more done, with better results, in less time.

Exhibit 6. Planning and executing two similar groups of projects with different time distributions.

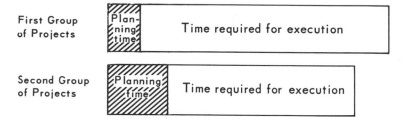

First Group of Projects — Plan-ning time — Time required for execution

Second Group of Projects — Planning time — Time required for execution

SOURCE: R. Alec Mackenzie, *Managing Time at the Top* (New York: The Presidents Association, 1970). Copyright © 1970 by The Presidents Association. Reprinted by permission.

THE TYRANNY OF THE URGENT

Urgency engulfs the manager; yet the most urgent task is not always the most important. The tyranny of the urgent lies in its distortion of priorities—its subtle cloaking of minor

projects with major status, often under the guise of "crisis."
One of the measures of a manager is his ability to distinguish
the important from the urgent, to refuse to be tyrannized by
the urgent, to refuse to manage by crisis.

Strangely, one of the major reasons for failure to plan is that
putting out today's fires is given priority over planning for tomorrow, thus insuring an ample supply of kindling to be con-
sumed in future fires. Charles Hummel observes:

> The important task rarely must be done today, or even this
> week. The urgent task calls for instant action. The momentary ap-
> peal of these tasks seems irresistible and they devour our energy.
> But in the light of time's perspective their deceptive prominence
> fades. With a sense of loss we recall the important tasks pushed
> aside. We realize we've become slaves to the tyranny of the ur-
> gent.[4]

Describing the harm that haste can do, Ralph Cordiner, as
president of General Electric, traced its cause to another stra-
tum of feeling:

> Worry is fundamentally a form of fear. It is a realization of inad-
> equacy, which in turn is the byproduct of lack of time to think
> through confidently to sound objectives and good plans. Hurry, in
> turn, is a parallel evidence of mismanagement of the specific and
> limited time available to the individual manager. It means that his
> work as a manager is poorly done because he is trying to do too
> many things in too few hours; and hence is doing them badly and
> thus is himself creating the vicious spiral of worry and the emo-
> tional strains which can only end in physical disaster.[5]

Various groups of managers have also tackled the causes of
the tyranny of the urgent. One interesting reason given by a
group in Montreal was "our own gratification in overcoming
crises." Because of this need, the group reasoned, managers
many times create their own crises. Another cause was identified in these terms: "Most of us think we work best under
pressure. Subconsciously we wait—delay, procrastinate—
until the pressure forces us into action. But do we really work
best under pressure, or do we work simply faster and less

well because of hasty judgments or lack of preparation? Is the problem deeper—a lack of internal motivation?"

Still another reason that fire fighting becomes necessary, according to Leo Moore, is the reluctance of subordinates to present bad news in the hope that it will get better before they have to report it.[6] The problem, of course, is that bad news often gets worse, as Lieutenant General Creighton Abrams discovered in Vietnam. The general was shocked and chagrined at one point in the conflict to discover that what he had been led to believe was a very favorable situation in fact was serious and rapidly deteriorating. "You people are telling me what you think I want to know," he stormed. "I want to know what is actually happening." [7]

A group of Canadian managers recommended that executives anticipate crises by planning only 80 percent of the day, leaving 20 percent unplanned to provide a cushion for the unexpected. Another strategy is contingency planning. After a crisis resulting from conditions that can reasonably be expected to recur, the effective manager thinks through what steps can be taken to prevent these conditions from developing into a crisis again.

Roger Morrison defines crisis management as coping with problems as they arise. "Companies throughout the world," he maintains, "have failed to recognize that they must manage their business, rather than be managed by it. Too often management feels that its job is to cope with problems as they arise ('crisis management') rather than to anticipate the problems and to take steps to mitigate their impact." [8]

Essential Steps in Planning

Essentially the planning process involves (1) analyzing the present situation (where I am now), (2) developing relevant assumptions (what conditions are likely to exist within the time span of the plan), (3) establishing objectives (what I want to achieve), (4) developing alternatives (what different ways might attain these objectives), (5) making and implementing the decision, and (6) establishing review and control procedures.

Many managers, neglecting to look ahead, allow their tasks to get pushed together and thus find themselves running out of time. Since pressure usually mounts with the level in management, it seems logical to assume that this tendency is often most pronounced among presidents. While few will quarrel with the concept that planning for the future is the heart of the chief executive's responsibility, most will admit that the pressure of events conspires to prevent their fulfilling this principal task. A Daniel Howard survey of 179 chief executives confirms this observation: it found that 83 percent of those responding didn't have time to keep up with the reading essential to their field and 72 percent complained they hadn't time to think or to plan.[9]

Yet who is to blame for this condition? Isn't the chief executive the one person empowered to control his own circumstances? Who else in the organization has ultimate authority? Who else has the power to assign responsibilities in order to free himself to do the things he ought to do?

A highly revealing look at a day of a chief executive is recounted by Joseph Cooper. It is the description given him by Charles Percy of one of his days as president of Bell and Howell. He reviewed how his day used to go, often quite frustratingly. Then he outlined what actions he took to organize himself and how he operated under his new arrangements.

When Percy first assumed the presidency of Bell and Howell, he observed, "I was so busy doing things I should have delegated I didn't have time to manage." Watching the flood of events focusing steady and unrelenting pressures on his job, he came to realize that the man should run the job rather than the reverse. He began consciously to divert time from the immediately urgent to the ultimately important. In this process his secretary played a key role by undertaking such tasks as screening, handling, or drafting responses to practically all mail. Many phone calls he received involved areas of responsibility directly assigned to other officers. Percy had

the executive involved call back to ask if he could be of service. Percy found that to accept such calls not only unnecessarily eroded his own day but also curtailed the responsible
officer's authority.

He determined the areas or functions most important to his
job: (1) planning for the future of the company, (2) coordinating the various divisions and functions of the company,
and (3) participating in civic activities as a representative of
the company. Then he delegated all other tasks and responsibilities.

His planning was reflected in his having all but emergency
calls during the morning held until just after lunch. When
making the calls then (at a time of his own choosing), he
often got routine mail and other documents signed. He was
better prepared for the calls, being advised of their purpose,
and made them briefer since he was conscious of how many
there were to be completed.

Since the typical day described often left little time for
long-range planning, he held periodic day-long sessions with
top officers for planning purposes away from the plant and
out of reach of telephones.

Percy concluded that effective use of his day required intelligent handling of the demands on his time. Now a United
States Senator, he finds the same management principle ap-
plies. "Without planning, organizing, and delegating effectively," he says, "no manager can long succeed in any
endeavor." [10]

PROTECT YOUR TIME

Many executives do *not* read their mail first. Instead they
deliberately have it held until they get a number of important
matters settled. This is particularly advantageous where, as
most often seems to be the case, the mail rarely holds really
top-priority matters.

The "quiet hour" was designed to provide the opportunity
for the uninterrupted concentration so crucial to executive
effectiveness. Dwane Bower, of Michigan Millers Insurance

Company, describes how the policy works in his company. No outgoing phone calls, no paging, no unnecessary talking, no excessive movement: these are the guidelines. More than 90 percent of the employees find they improve concentration and organization of their work when they are free from interruptions. Of course there are exceptions, as in the case of new employees who need to consult with their supervisors or field men who are heading out on assignment and need instructions.

Flagrant violators are reprimanded by their supervisors, but as a rule this isn't necessary, according to Bower. In fact, some department heads have found the period so profitable that they have extended it beyond company policy by adding a second quiet hour or half-hour immediately after lunch.

A manager would not long be successful if he treated his financial, material, and other resources as he does his time. Even United States Presidents have had to take action to protect their time. By executive order in 1939, Franklin D. Roosevelt created the Executive Office of the President "to protect the President's time by excluding any matter that can be settled elsewhere." This mechanism evolved into a group of assistants and counselors who stand between the President and almost all incoming communications. They decide (1) *what*—which matters should be brought to the President's attention, (2) *by whom*—by the originator or a White House aide, (3) *how*—by letter or verbal communication, and (4) *when*.[11]

The principle of decision level should accomplish for managers what this executive order accomplishes for Presidents of the United States. When decisions are made at the lowest level possible (where required information and judgment are available), then matters that *can* be settled elsewhere *will* be. Effective executives will settle for nothing less.

Setting Objectives and Goals

For purposes of the present discussion, "objectives" mean the accomplishments sought by an organization over a long run,

and "goals" mean short-range aims. In most enterprises a time
span in excess of one year designates a plan as long range
and less than a year as short range. The terms "strategic" and
"operational" often coincide with these respective time
projections. Thus one may speak of "strategic planning of
long-range objectives" and "operational planning of short-
range goals."

The increasing popularity of managing-by-objectives
(MBO) programs speaks to the critical nature of objectives.
The use of objectives in management undoubtedly far exceeds
the use of formalized terminology. For example, the General
Electric Management Institute has avoided the term "MBO."
Yet when asked if GE has ever been managed *without* consideration of objectives, any officer of the insitute will unhesi-
tatingly answer no. The monumental four-volume *Professional Management in General Electric* designates planning
as the first function of the professional manager and determining objectives as the first activity of planning.

THE MYTH OF EFFICIENCY

When goals and objectives are being set either for a company or for an individual, it is important to avoid overstress-
ing efficiency and neglecting the careful selection of areas in
which efficiency ought to be sought. The "myth of efficiency"
lies in the assumption that the most efficient manager is ipso
facto the most effective; actually, the most efficient manager
working on the wrong task will not be effective. Auren Uris
cautions executives against the "hazard" of emphasizing efficiency without regard to results.[12] When long-range objectives become obscured it is easy to replace them with much
shorter-range and even hopelessly misplaced goals, such as
efficiency. This is not to argue against being efficient in the
right things at the right time. But efficiency, as an end in
itself, is futile.

The allure of efficiency may seem almost irresistible. It's
like motherhood—who would be against it? But take a case
in point: expending effort most efficiently on reducing the

unit costs of a product that is close to the end of its life cycle. Efficient action that puts method ahead of results, that disregards planned objectives, may be totally ineffective and may have to be done again. Hence the slogan: If you don't have time to do it right, when will you have time to do it over? Choosing between doing a job right and doing the right job poses no problem for the effective executive.

Setting Priorities

Time does not permit the manager to do all the things that his conscience or imagination tells him he might, says F. D. Barrett. Whether the executive's week runs 40, 60, or 80 hours appears to make no difference. The proportion of can-do to might-do activities remains small. Barrett concludes that the solution to the problem of time management lies in a direction profoundly different from the simple expedient of long hours.[13]

One hesitates to suggest to otherwise intelligent and highly successful executives that rather than working longer hours they simply ought to decide what to do and not do. Yet why should one assume that high office presupposes immunity from the problems of how best to allocate limited supplies of time? Former Secretary of State Dean Acheson was in an excellent position to observe high government officials and to assess their utilization of time. He observed:

No one knows better than I that the published appointment list of the president or a cabinet officer is only that one-tenth of the iceberg which appears above water. But even a short study of the sample given makes two points clear: first, at least half the appointments are wholly unnecessary, and second, those which are necessary are neither very time-consuming nor exhausting.[14]

The trouble with our country, said Lyndon Johnson during his White House days, is that we constantly put second things first. He might as well have spoken for managers, housewives, workers, students, professionals, salesmen—in fact, for everyone. We all put second things first by default.

This isn't so bad—but if we get down to putting the twenty-second thing first, we are in trouble.

Check yourself. The last time you approached your desk to start something new, what did you select? Did you think through your priorities and consciously select the most important? Or did you allow your attention to move to the item most interesting at the moment or the one your gaze happened to fall on or the one brought up by a drop-in visitor? Of course we often do the more interesting with the rationalization that getting it out of the way will clear the decks for the more important task. Ever spend all day "getting organized" so you could "get to work" on the important task, only to find the time gone and nothing but inconsequentials attended to? This is a common trap, most difficult to avoid.

Top executives are not alone in having difficulty establishing priorities. While everyone agrees they are important for the nation as well as for each individual, few have considered carefully how to set them. The question is how to determine which of the array of undone and emerging tasks is really first. By what criteria do we judge? An assistant principal of a junior high school looked me straight in the eye and said, "I don't have a No. 1 priority—I have 30 of them on my desk right now!"

W. Dickerson Hogue, a senior lecturer in international business at Indiana University, has made a useful contribution to the analysis of priorities. He cites a hypothetical conclusion of a conference. The president of the company says, "Let's be sure we all agree on priorities on the projects we've discussed." His four top executives all agree that the priority should be project A first, followed by projects B, C, and D.

In reality, says Hogue, they may be speaking of four quite different types of priorities. One may be thinking in terms of "relative" priorities, with all four projects being worked on simultaneously but with more effort put on those higher in priority. He may feel that of 1,000 total man-hours available per month, project A should have 400 per month until finished, B 300, C 200, and D 100. Moreover, even if everyone agrees that relative priority is the sort intended, there is considerable room for misunderstanding on the *degrees* of priority. The man-hours might be distributed 800, 100, 75, and 25 or in any other combination of decreasing magnitudes adding up to 1,000.

A second person may feel that spill-over priority is intended—that all available effort should be put on the top-priority project until it is completed, then on the next highest, and so on. Thus he will think that project A should be allocated 1,000 man-hours per month until finished, then project B should have the full allotment, and so forth.

A third executive may view the intended distribution of effort as subject to modification in case of conflict. All projects will be worked on with equal effort unless some type of conflict arises among them, in which case the higher-ranking project will always be favored over any of the others. Thus at the outset each of four projects will be given 250 of the 1,000 available man-hours apiece. Then if A should lose any of its manpower, the loss will be made up from D's manpower. Or if B and D both want to use the only available pilot plant on Wednesday, B will be entitled to preference over D.

Still another person may favor a ranking that establishes the order of completion while allowing some progress simultaneously on all projects. Project A should be the first finished and D the last. He may feel that a reasonable distribution of man-hours would be 150 per month for project A (enough to finish first), 500 for B (to finish second), 50 for C (to finish third), and 300 for D (to finish fourth).

A building contractor who tells his on-site foreman that excavation has the first priority and pouring the foundation walls the second clearly means completion priority. A sales manager who says his men are giving top priority this month to pushing a given product means relative priority.[15]

THE PARETO PRINCIPLE

The Pareto principle, named after the nineteenth-century Italian economist and sociologist Vilfredo Pareto, states that the significant items in a given group normally constitute a relatively small portion of the total items in the group. Since an executive's most important problems as well as opportunities are concentrated, the wisdom of focused effort is apparent. The principle of concentration is not new. Military logistics have always called for the use of a force superior to that of the enemy at the decisive point and the critical time. Many naval battles in history have been won by numerically inferior forces. The typical battle plan called for teams of ships to concentrate on isolating the enemy's vessels and destroying them one at a time. Equal or unfavorable encounters were to be avoided. Maneuvering was to be continued with one purpose in mind—achieving a temporary advantage through a concentration of power and delivering a fast knockout punch.

Joseph Juran, author and lecturer on management, first used the terms "vital few" and "trivial many" in applying the Pareto principle to a great variety of managerial situations.[16]

Exhibit 7. The Pareto time principle.

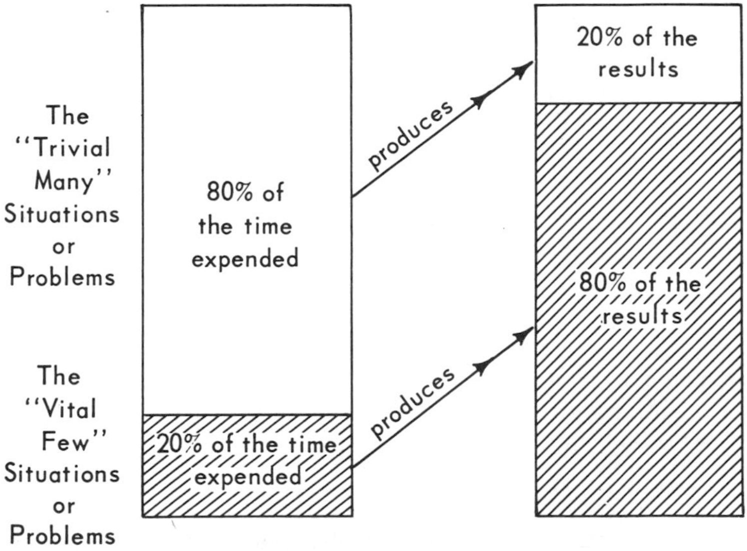

SOURCE: R. Alec Mackenzie, *Managing Time at the Top* (New York: The Presidents Association, 1970). Copyright © 1970 by The Presidents Association. Reprinted by permission.

Exhibit 7 illustrates his useful analysis of this principle. The percentages reflect the discovery, by American project engineers who applied the Pareto principle to inventory control, that 20 percent of the items normally comprise about 80 percent of the value of a given inventory. Efforts to control the "vital few" elements brought results out of all proportion to the efforts expended.

An insurance company that had never segregated its sales accounts by relative size decided this would be a good idea. It discovered that less than 10 percent of its accounts represented nearly 90 percent of its total sales volume. Yet its overall efforts in selling and servicing accounts had never been targeted on this small but vitally important group. A radical policy change resulted in significant gains in sales and profits for the ensuing year directly attributable to this approach.

Auren Uris describes a company that asked its officers to list the obstacles to increasing profitability. The list totaled 37 problems—too many to handle at once. It was returned to its drafters with the request that they rank the problems in order of importance. The revised list showed only five matters falling into the category of the "vital few." Uris also tells how the president of a clock-making company eliminated one-third of the regular models when he found they added up to only 4 percent of the company's sales volume. Within six months the firm was doing a larger and more profitable volume.[17]

MANAGING BY EXCEPTION

Management by exception is based on the Pareto principle. It holds that only significant deviations of actual from planned performance should be reported to the responsible executive to conserve his time, energy, and ability.[18] When first proposed as a doctrine for effective management, it was widely thought to be a simple statement of the obvious. Yet if it is so obvious, why is it practiced so little? And if many of the sounder practices of management, both anticipatory and remedial, are based on some form of exception management, why is it not more readily recognized and discussed?

Companies that are aware of the problem of overcommunication through unnecessary memos and reports usually resort to some form of exception management. They often reduce the size of reports by requiring that only data indicating deviations from normal be included. Specifically omitted are voluminous statistics on conditions that present no problems and in effect simply reflect performance in accordance with plan.

I was visiting with one of the directors of a large European consulting firm. On the corner of his desk lay a sizable computer printout. In response to my inquiry, he explained that it reported the status of all projects in the firm. Since this firm had more than 100 professionals, each engaged in a number of projects, the size of the material was substantial. I asked the director if he read the printouts. He responded, "Are you kidding? Why do you think I have them placed right over the wastebasket?"

The efforts of chief executives to redirect their managers' attention from "administrivia" to the "vital few" tasks will show itself in managerial effectiveness that may be multiplied many times.

DECIDING WHAT NOT TO DO

Jay W. Forrester, professor of industrial management at Massachusetts Institute of Technology, estimates that middle management's lifetime effectiveness is as low as one-tenth of the theoretical maximum. However, he points out, "Insofar as lifetime performance is concerned, an individual literally need make only *one* significant contribution in his whole 40 years of service to raise his rating from an average 10 percent to say 50 percent or better." [19]

Most consultants who have considered the average effectiveness of managers would tend to rate it in the area of 30 percent. What an overall improvement of 10 percent across the board could produce is something to contemplate. Moving the average to only 40 percent would represent a one-third improvement in effectiveness.

Concerning priorities, Herman Krannert has observed, "I sometimes like to measure a man by the things he decides to leave undone. The man who insists on getting 100 percent of his job done either doesn't have enough to do or doesn't have the kind of stuff it takes to succeed in business today."[20]

Perhaps no one summed up the essence of priorities better than Newbold Noyes, of *The Washington Star*. In discussing his strategy for replacing *The Washington Post* as the capital's leading newspaper, he said, "The *Star* will not try to do everything. That requires no judgment. We want to decide what is important and cover those aspects well."

Refusing to do the unimportant is a requisite for success, says Frank Nunlist. Chief executives must stay out of day-to-day operations if they are to have time to plan for the future. Too many managers, says Nunlist, carry superfluous information with them as they move up the ladder. They must learn how to forget the unnecessary and to ignore the irrelevant.[21]

In a similar vein Curtis Symonds emphasizes that management "has a very basic need *not to know*. It has a need to be protected from the mass of operating detail which a typical information system can provide; . . . from information that does not inform; from details on which no action can be taken; from the exact manner in which delegated authority has been exercised."[22] Symonds concludes that management must free itself of nonessential data to fulfill its role of managing—a process often subordinated to the more routine tasks of administration.

LEARNING TO SAY NO

The problems people have with priorities vary. Some find it hard to set them but don't seem to encounter many problems in honoring them. Others may have little trouble setting them but a great deal carrying them out. Most managers probably experience some difficulty on both counts.

Sorting priorities may be particularly hard under pressure conditions with events changing rapidly and critical factors shifting constantly. In such circumstances the ability to determine priorities, focus efforts, maintain concentration, and persevere is rare indeed.

One observer noted that our problem is not usually with priorities "one to three . . . rather it is with posteriorities four to infinity." Every project, every priority has an advocate somewhere. No one has described this phenomenon more vividly than Theodore Levitt:

> Relentless pressure is beamed at the president from his lieutenants in each department, each constantly telling him that his direct, personal support is needed immediately lest the enterprise suffer irreparable harm. The chief's sympathetic and undeviating attention is demanded for production, finance, personnel, community relations, labor relations, R&D and, of course, marketing. If the poor man responded fully, he would scarcely have time to be president! [23]

Every project is on somebody's must list. Because managers do not like to say no, they establish priorities and then add "just a little bit" of 85 other things, ending up getting nothing done. One simply cannot achieve excellence of performance without concentrating effort on the critical areas. Therefore one has to say about a suggested but secondary project, "This is very nice but it's not our first priority. If it must be done, we'll have to let somebody else do it."

Learn to say no. Let somebody else do it. "Over the years," said Robert Updegraff, "I have listened to people complain about not having time for the things they ought to do or would like to do and I have discovered that many of them suffer from a common trouble: they are timid about using the greatest time-saving word in the English language, the little two-letter word NO." [24]

The Plan Sheet at Economics Laboratory

E. B. Osborn, president of Economics Laboratory, Inc., in New York, has gone farther than most chief executives in orienting his firm toward highly effective time management. In this company, managing time is very close in meaning to managing the job.

One of the most important methods used for managing the job at Economics Laboratory is the plan sheet. The plan sheet is the principal topic of discussion in the company's *Executive Development Manual,* written by President Osborn. This guide is made available to all managers, but they are told that what they do with it is up to them. (In a separate interview another EL executive said, "There isn't a man in the company who is not using it.")

The first objective of the plan sheet is to furnish the executive with a tool for self-management. The manual states:

One quality that has brought many executives up to their present positions has been their ability to handle emergencies and to work under pressure. But an executive, in order to endure and grow, will soon find it imperative to concentrate on the elimination of emergencies; he will need to learn, as his responsibilities increase, what he will do himself, what he will do first, and what he will not do at all.

The manual continues:

The plan sheet, simply stated, is a means of organizing one's thinking and planning all in one place and in the least amount of time with [a] maximum degree of thoroughness. Even before the use of this tool has been mastered, an executive will find he is handling, in an unhurried and unharried manner, a greater volume of work smoothly and efficiently. As training in this technique is extended to all levels of management, the benefit to the individual, to the reputation of his department, and to the profitable operation of the company must be self-evident. . . .

The plan sheet . . . fits any job where there is more than one single function to perform. The only person who will have no use for it is the man on the assembly line. For the secretary, her desk calendar will serve the purpose. For most executives with broader responsibilities, more space is needed—in simplest terms, a sheet of paper listing all the things he intends to handle or anything he wants to remember. . . .

The plan sheet is never intended to be used for the time "when I am cleaned up"; it is designed to get the executive out from under when things are at their worst, and to give him the feeling that the many facets and details of his operation are under control. . . . By using the plan sheet to set up priorities, an executive can

Exhibit 8. An Economics Laboratory plan sheet.

Plan Sheet for 7/3

PHONING

② Sheraton – Tate Ⓟ (phone flap)
   Keeler – lunch
③ Wallace – see about safe dep. box
   Hill – on meeting Ⓟ
④ D.W. Jones – re Friday date
① J.A. Smith – see at 10:00?
   Call home – re Saturday
   Reservations for Florida Ⓟ

WRITING

⑤ Item Ⓦ
   " Ⓦ
   " Ⓦ
   " Ⓦ
   " Ⓦ
⑥ Dictate to 10:00 A.M. –
   mail received last night

GENERAL

Item Ⓓ
" Ⓓ Ⓓ
" Ⓓ
Study for meeting with R&D

MEETINGS

New prod. – NY 8/22	Mon.
J.A. Smith – Tues.	Tues.
With R&D – 8/20	Wed.
Exec. develop. 8/28 –	Thurs.
3:00 P.M.	Fri.

LUNCHES

7/3	Mon.	7/10	
7/4	Tues.	7/11	
7/5	Wed.	7/12	
7/6	Thurs.	7/13	
7/7	Fri.	7/14	

⑦ **J.A. SMITH**

Item
" ①
" ②
" ③
" ⑤
" ⑥
" ④

D.W. JONES

Item
" ⑨
"
"

F.J. CARLTON

Item
" ⑧
"
"
"
"

W.M. PALMER

Item
"
"
"
"

have the satisfaction of knowing that the most urgent matters will be disposed of. The unpredictable and often unavoidable interruptions that do occur will not ruffle him, and he will waste little time wondering "where was he" before they happened.

A plan sheet can be as unique and distinctive to an individual as that individual is himself. The important thing is that it serve its essential purpose of recording and organizing the unfinished and future business of an executive, which even the most brilliant memory expert could not hope to carry in an orderly and fool-proof fashion in his head.

Any executive's work can be categorized under the headings of *phoning, writing, general, meetings, lunches,* and the *names* of colleagues routinely worked with. The first five are normally carried on the first sheet of legal-sized paper [see Exhibit 8] . . . a margin is left for checking and numbering. On subsequent sheets (normally only one) are listed the names of colleagues with whom there are to be discussions. Printed under each man's name are the topics that are accumulated prior to a scheduled meeting. . . .

Items to be listed under *phoning* are self-evident. When the secretary retypes a fresh plan sheet (either weekly or whenever it becomes filled up), she will omit whatever has been crossed out under this category. It is recommended that because of the huge number of phone calls, covering everything from talks with outsiders to those you want to phone internally, they be printed in small letters and in pencil. The reason for this is that this category becomes quickly filled if properly used, and when it is filled erasures are easy with space thus provided for additional reminders to yourself of calls you wish to make and without requiring retyped plan sheets too frequently.

Under *writing,* however, only those items should be listed which will not be dictated immediately, either because of a need for further information or because no dictation time is available that day. When there is a large accumulation of mail to be answered (such as occurs following a trip out of town), this space is not used, because it would be inadequate and because usually "the pile" is tackled all at one time on a day set aside for that purpose. The bulk of an ordinary day's mail is handled quickly and handled

SOURCE FOR EXHIBIT 8: R. Alec Mackenzie, *Managing Time at the Top* (New York: The Presidents Association, 1970). Reprinted by permission. Based on a sample plan sheet in E. B. Osborn, *Executive Development Manual* (New York: Economics Laboratory, Inc., September 1959).

daily; otherwise an executive cannot hope to keep on top of his job. Each item that is deferred, even though necessarily, automatically requires more time to answer, because the writer must refresh his memory on the subject and re-create (in his reply) the thoughts he had when he first read the item.

Routinely, the matters to be handled under *phoning* and *writing* are scheduled for the first hour and a half in the morning. . . .

The first hour and a half in the morning has been mentioned as the best time for disposing of correspondence [and] telephone calls—and trying to anticipate interruptions, whether by telephone or by someone "sticking [his] head in the door for just a minute." It should not be hard to see, except where a real emergency exists and minutes are precious, that the plan sheet can avoid the great majority of these spontaneous interruptions and is thus a management tool designed to protect every member of the executive group. When each man knows that the other is trying to follow a preplanned program, a little thought will usually show that the question that just occurred to him, or an item of news he is bursting to pass on, can be listed under the person's name for attention at an agreed upon time.[25]

Osborn summarizes his discussion of the plan sheet by providing four important tips: (1) keep the plan sheet current; (2) always schedule the most important subjects for handling first, numbering them in order of not just importance or priority but when they will fit best and be best executed; (3) never yield to the temptation to clean up "small" items first, which he describes as the pathway to frustration; and (4) comb the plan sheet for items that can be delegated.

Chapter 4

Getting

Organized

"If your aim is control," E. B. Osborn has said, "it must be self-control first. If your aim is management, it must be self-management first. Beside the task of acquiring the ability to organize a day's work, all else you will ever learn about management is but child's play." [1]

No one has put it more succinctly. Organizing a day's work has never been known as the easiest job the manager faces, but how many have pinpointed it as perhaps the most difficult? We confront this task more regularly than any other. Still, few of us recognize how hard it really is or how poorly we execute it. "One of my biggest problems," a college administrator told me, "is organizing for getting organized."

In a discussion on the awakening interest in time management for executives, Palle Hansen, head of the Institute for Leadership, Copenhagen, was recollecting with interest the early emphasis on time study in production. "Isn't it strange," he ventured, "that with all the time, money, and work we have put into analyzing the effectiveness of our efforts in the plant, we have paid so little attention to the much more costly efforts in our executive offices?"

We talked about the reasons for this neglect—among them the reluctance of managers, who have the final say, to submit to measurement; the less structured nature of their tasks; and the relative difficulty of measuring many of the sought-for results. Yet, as we shall see, the times are demanding ways, and they are being found, to help executives achieve more effective time management. It is becoming increasingly clear that the profit squeeze encountered during the recession of the early 1970s will propel a continuing and more rigorous review of the effectiveness of managerial efforts.

Organizing the Work Space

"Like all other craftsmen," said Sune Carlson, "executives are dependent on their working environment." [2] A senior officer of a large company was giving serious thought to managing his time better. Our discussion ranged across a wide variety of time wasters. Principal among these was his failure to have his secretary screen calls and visitors effectively. It was not until we looked at the physical location of his office and his secretary's desk that we realized how locked into his situation he really was.

In the company's massive international headquarters building, the private secretaries were typically clustered in pools near the corners. As a result, this officer's secretary was physically some 30 feet from his office door. Any hope of having visitors screened was futile. And since the main corridor passed directly by his office door, the opportunities for his friends to stick their heads in to say hello were legion. To compound this situation, the corporate headquarters had an open-door policy which, though never forcefully articulated, was nonetheless felt to be more or less obligatory. But certainly conforming to this policy was never meant to make a manager the victim of the drop-in interruption. I felt the officer's frustration as he described a typical occurrence:

"You feel a presence. You glance up and sure enough there it is. A more or less disembodied head poked around the door jamb. I grin and nod to acknowledge its presence. It grins back and reciprocates with a nod. A few remarks are exchanged, and as often as not the body follows the head into my office, and another friend has dropped in for a chat."

Of course the officer can simply close the door. Some managers have solved this problem by placing their desk so that they do not immediately face the door, turning it so that they sit at a right angle or even with their back to the door. This helps them control the compulsion to look up to see who the "presence" is.

The third and far preferable solution is to position one's secretary in front of the door to make it virtually impossible for a visitor to enter without checking with her. The diplomatic skills of the secretary in minimizing drop-in interruptions are naturally of paramount importance.

With respect to the location of subordinates, those talked to most frequently ought to be nearby. Physical propinquity is a very real factor in determining frequency of communication. Being in a different part of the building or on a different floor is a significant contact barrier. One top executive deliberately moved two division heads to another floor to encourage them to work more independently. At the same time he placed two others near his office because he needed close contact with them for his own work.

OFFICE LANDSCAPING TO REDUCE DISTRACTIONS

If you had glanced at the central office of the Facit International Headquarters, in Atvidaberg, Sweden, before its "landscaping," you might not have given it a second thought. Looking more attentively, you might have noticed that there were calculating machines and typewriters at most of the desks. Then you might have wondered whether the desks' proximity to each other caused some problems because of the unavoidable noise of the machines.

The landscaping of the headquarters has created radically

different surroundings: a symphony of cheerful colors, carefully selected and blended for the most pleasing impact; a feeling of separateness because of low, angular partitions with decorative round holes in them to provide airiness and visibility; a quietness resulting from the soundproofing. Interruptions have been reduced, concentration is easier, and morale has risen.

When I compare this scene mentally with the physical environment found in the offices of a United States corporation engaged in somewhat similar work, the contrast is striking. The complaints of the American engineers ranged from "unavoidable interruptions by every passerby" through "a holocaust of noise from the paging system" to "telephones on neighboring desks that ring on and on even though unanswered."

As necessary as sustained concentration is to executive performance, the control of surrounding noise has become mandatory. Major corporations began moving their research and development facilities into the relative quiet of the suburbs more than a decade ago, recognizing that undisturbed surroundings are also highly desirable for research-oriented work.

The United States company just mentioned is now considering a number of solutions to its noise problems, such as paging selectively rather than at random, using more pleasant voices over the system, and strictly limiting the number of people to be paged. Even more interesting is a proposal to convert a little-used room into a quiet retreat for study and review. The firm is also considering the possibility of dividing a relatively large room into smaller segments.

THE FUNCTIONAL OFFICE

Professional firms have made a study of how to make offices more functional. Diagrams are drawn of work flow so that travel patterns and the location of work stations, files, and desks can be strategically designed.

For the manager at his desk as well as the secretary at

hers, the handy location of equipment and supplies in greatest demand is essential. Such a simple item as a shoulder support for the telephone becomes an extremely useful tool for the manager who finds it desirable while calling to work with both hands, whether to pull a file and turn quickly to a needed document or simply to jot down notes with greater ease.

Generally speaking, all personnel at all levels should have the best equipment the enterprise can afford to get the job done. Since manpower usually constitutes the greatest single operating expense, the investment in the necessary machinery to do the best possible job is sound. Poor, obsolete, or broken-down equipment usually requires a great deal of adjusting, and the resulting down time produces slowdowns that are ultimately more expensive than new and reliable equipment.

Uncomfortable seating and dim or flickering lighting can lead to physical fatigue, which reduces personal productivity. Office illumination should be evenly distributed and free from glare and shadows but strong enough to light an entire desk. Replacing a secretarial chair that does not provide the proper back support may be one of the most valuable investments a manager can make with respect to the productivity of his office.

DESKS AND THEIR USES

A neighbor of mine has taken the most advanced step in making a desk functional that I have yet heard about. He wanted his desk completely equipped, including chairs for his visitors. He designed his own executive desk with all the modern conveniences plus one creative innovation—with a flick of a switch, one or two chairs, depending on the number of guests, appears on the far side.

Lawrence Appley, during his years as president of the American Management Association, was one of the first to experiment with the idea of the chief executive having no desk at all. The idea behind this move was that the desk can be a formidable barrier to effective communication between a boss and a subordinate. Comfortable chairs arranged casually around a coffee table seemed to inspire ease of communication. A second thought voiced by those who liked the idea was that it provided no place for a subordinate to leave his problems—thus delegating them upward; what was brought in was also carried out. However, a possible flaw in the no-desk arrangement is that the comfortable and relaxed atmosphere it creates could tend to prolong meetings. One manager told me he uses both a regular desk and a coffee table. If he wants a short meeting, he stays behind his regular desk.

Perhaps the most interesting "innovation" in desks is not an innovation at all. The stand-up desk is probably one of the oldest ideas around. When Harry Morgan was special assistant to DeWitt Wallace, the founder-owner of *Reader's Digest*, he described his stand-up desk as a very effective alternative for certain types of work; he welcomed the change to standing on his feet while moving ahead on a project. It occurred to me as we talked that many times I find myself wanting to stand up and walk around in the middle of a conversation. When the situation permits, I frequently do so. It seems to break the structure of the conversation and thus to give me a slightly different perspective on the matter under consideration.

THE STACKED-DESK SYNDROME

In my experience the stacked-desk syndrome afflicts more than 95 percent of all managers. For a number of years, when discussing this problem with other managers, I had approached it as self-descriptive and well-defined—all that was wanting was a solution. Such a casual approach needs no comment. Mistaken or imprecise problem identification lies at the root of a great deal of managerial ineffectiveness.

It took an older manager with a sense of humor to focus my attention on the causes of the stacked desk. With a twinkle in his eye, this German executive asked one day whether I really had thought about how desks get stacked. Then he volunteered: "It's because of all the things we don't want to forget. The things we want to remember we put on top of our desk, where we will see them. The problem is," he continued, "that it really works. Every time our gaze wanders and we look at them, we remember them and our train of thought is broken. Then as the stacks grow higher, we are unable to remember what's beneath the top, so we begin to look for things in the stacks. So time is wasted both in retrieving lost items and in the interruptions occasioned by looking at all the items we didn't want to forget!"

Someone has said, "Cluttered desk—cluttered mind." When Ralph Cordiner was asked about the clean desk for which he was famous, the inquirer received a swift response: "Why shouldn't it be? Isn't one important thing enough to be doing at a time? It makes it easier to finish one task without being interrupted by another."

Taking the following steps is one helpful method of uncluttering a desk and keeping it so:

1. Clear your desk of everything related in any way to projects other than the one at hand. That one ought to be your top priority for the moment.°

2. Do not permit any other items to be put on your desk until you are ready for them. This means that all projects must have a place in a file or drawer and ought to be in that place.

3. Resist temptations to leave the project you are working on for other, more appealing tasks, because of attractive interruptions, or because you are tired of it. Be sure you have taken all possible action indicated before disposing of it.

4. Send it on its way, recheck your priorities, then start on the next most important project.

5. Have standing orders with your secretary to see that the desk is cleared before you arrive in the morning and that

---

° If you have trouble keeping track of your priorities, try the plan sheet that has solved the problem at Economics Laboratory (Exhibit 8 in the preceding chapter).

the material necessary for starting on the No. 1 priority for the day is on your desk.

6. Make it a continuous responsibility for your secretary to inspect your desk and continue to keep it clear. Cooperate with her in every way possible to make this easy.

While the method outlined above has proved effective for many managers, it may not be suitable for all and in fact may be a stumbling block to some. For instance, uncluttering a desk one item at a time could turn into a fetish, and an executive may become so frustrated if a single sheet of paper is out of place that he will be unable to work. Thus, as with all guidelines, it is important that the rules be adapted to individual needs.

Whatever method one chooses, however, unpiling the desk has proved valuable even to people who thrive on stacks. K. R. Hinckley, of Houston Lighting & Power Company, wrote in a letter:

> I have always had an operating style of having things piled on my desk within arm's reach—to save time. Material piles are arranged for urgency—one stack for things to do as soon as possible; another for semi-urgent matters; another for "can wait until you get around to it"; another for leisure reading, etc. Generally this does make for a messy-looking shop and the various stacks are, indeed, distracting. However, I was tickled to death last year when I got a larger desk, for it provided more space for more piles. After the seminar, however, I moved some of the piles out of reach and immediate sight over to my coffee table and credenza. You were right; the ready distraction has been eliminated. I do spend a little more time getting up and going to look for something that is semi-urgent or not so urgent. This disadvantage, however, is offset by the advantage that my coffee table and my credenza are more interesting-looking now.

All of which reminds me: without a sense of humor, we are destined to pretty dull days, aren't we?

WASTEBASKETRY

The art of wastebasketry has been designated by at least one management consultant as the most critical skill in managing one's work. The effective executive fights the tendency to overfile, realizing that it is costly both in time and in space.

In the film *Time to Think,* produced by The Rank Organisation Ltd., London, a manager demonstrates a relatively simple and direct approach to the problem of paperwork. His dictum for the mass of unimportant details that accumulate in the in basket: "Get rid of the bloody stuff as quickly as possible." He demonstrates his accuracy with the kind of paper that ought to be discarded immediately in the wastebasket. "Over the years," he explains, "I've developed quite an aim."

Auren Uris calls it putting-the-most-into-your-wastebasket. "Obviously," he says, "the basket you use should be big enough for all you can feed it. And it should be convenient to your hand, rather than occupy a spot determined by the whim of your maintenance people or even your secretary." [3]

The really hard decision in wastebasketry precedes the avalanche of paperwork. That is the decision on which materials ought to come into your desk and which ought to be screened out mercilessly by your secretary. As Frank Nunlist described it during his tenure as assistant postmaster general for operations, "Many managers find themselves reading this stuff coming into their in box in order to determine whether they ought to be reading it at all."

The Filing System

The attempt to solve the paper problem will be short-lived if the problem of how and what to file has not been mastered. I find that in enterprise after enterprise no common filing system has been established.

All too frequently the filing procedure is left to the manager's own whim. Usually he approaches it without the benefit of professional training and, depending on his tenure in the job, perhaps without even an idea of what main subject areas are required for effective interoffice communication in the handling of his major tasks. Thus it is obvious that the establishment of a filing system should not be left completely to the individual manager. Instead he should delegate the job to the person trained and qualified to do it, and except in large corporations (where file clerks are employed), that person is his secretary.

A secretary in the office of a senior Representative in Congress told me, "To begin with, the filing system is so complex as to render it ineffective for any of the staff other than the three of us who have access to it. And the three of us have never coordinated the way we file things."

A poor filing system is a constant irritation to staff people and a monumental time waster in terms of retrieving information. The importance of a uniform approach becomes eminently clear when absences require substitutions. Secretaries take vacations, fall sick, and are away on personal business from time to time just like all other employees. For these absences it is imperative that the filing system be understandable and the folders readily accessible. A uniform system insures that the same general subject headings are employed throughout an office for similar matters. A substitute secretary can rapidly retrieve needed materials if the files are set up the same way her own are. A diagram and guide sheet of the simplest nature should be quite adequate.

How does one know when to get rid of files? Experts in records retention have developed guidelines for the number of years that different types of documents ought to be saved. They suggest that the current operations files ought to include no more than one year of correspondence. When people in charge of office operations are asked to estimate the percentage of paperwork in the files that is *never* referred to again, estimates commonly range from 80 to 90 percent, and sometimes approach a staggering 95 to 99 percent. We should remember, however, that the retention of files is best determined not by arbitrary rules but by their use and importance.

Some papers should never go into the system, whereas others, such as those pertaining to legal matters, will rarely ever be removed.

Desk-organizing files, set up to catalog current tasks and items for followup, can be invaluable time savers and memory joggers. These will be described in Chapter 9. Many managers also find an idea file extremely useful. This is a convenient catchall for miscellaneous items or ideas not yet sufficiently developed to be categorized under a subject but interesting enough to warrant holding.

THE POCKET OR DESK DIARY

A single place for jotting down important ideas or information is a necessary auxiliary to the filing system. The most convenient device for this is a pocket or desk diary. Every manager at one time or another has found himself emptying his pockets of various notes on scraps of paper, three-by-five cards, or paper napkins from the restaurant where a luncheon meeting was held onto the top of his dresser in his bedroom. Some watch these notes accumulate for a month until the stack is so forbidding as to discourage even a tentative look. This form of nonmanagement leads to the certain loss of critical information and enormous time wasted in futile searches for misplaced notations.

The place to put something you may wish to retrieve at a future date is in a daily diary you keep with you or at your desk. This is the surest place to find the information or the event in question on the appropriate day. In addition, a sudden inspiration needn't interrupt your current work if you can write it down where you are confident you can find it; you can immediately forget it. Since adopting this system myself, I would hesitate to guess the number of man-weeks of time I have saved in fast retrieval of information desired.

Correspondence

Handling mail seems to be a far more personal matter to most executives than it ought to be. For example, it is not

uncommon for the entrepreneur, the self-made man who created the business and has nurtured it to real success, to insist
on continuing to open his own mail. He wants to keep his finger on the pulse of the business, and he may lack confidence
in the ability of subordinates to recognize the opportunities
and priorities in the mail. (It is typical of entrepreneurs to feel
that no one else could handle situations quite the way they
would.) Also some executives refuse to discipline their own
work habits in order to allow orderly procedures to take
place. Frank curiosity is another factor as is the desire to be
first to discover what's new—especially if it's good news.

Chicago's Dartnell Institute for Business Research surveyed
3,000 executives and found that the typical ones spent two to
three hours per day reading and answering mail. This is an
enormous investment of time—four months out of a year—in
handling correspondence.

The management team at Economics Laboratory finds that
the most orderly and least disruptive method of dealing with
mail not requiring immediate attention is to have it assembled at the end of the day and either given to the executive
to read on his way home or laid on his desk for early attention the following morning. This is better than the usual procedure of the secretary's taking the mail to the executive's
desk on delivery. The system does not clutter his desk, interrupt him, or distract his attention from matters before him. It
shields him from unplanned intrusions of information that
needlessly destroy his concentration and impede the momentum of his day.

Meshulan Riklis, whose entrepreneurship has been much
discussed in management circles, prefers to let all but the
most urgent mail mature in his in box for at least three
months. After this aging, he finds that 80 percent of it doesn't
need to be answered.[4]

SHORT, FAST ANSWERS

On the other hand, delayed responses do tend to get longer.
A few sentences will do for most memos and letters. Why

delay? The longer you wait the more compelled you will feel to give lengthy excuses.

Returning from a trip, my wife observed a businessman across the aisle from her in the airplane who pulled a thick sheaf of letters out of his briefcase a few minutes after boarding. He would read or scan a page, scribble something in the margin or at the top that must have been shorthand instructions to his secretary, and turn to the next item. He stayed on the job the whole flight—nearly three hours. My wife recalled that he got through an amazing stack of letters.

Now, my wife had several reasons for observing this incident so closely. I had already started work on this book. She knows that I have had difficulty arriving at a fixed procedure for the best handling of my own correspondence. And I do not always make the best use of my time on airplanes.

It is true that I would rarely have a stack of correspondence the size of the one she described. It is also true that in order to utilize a given time span effectively, some planning and preparation are required.

Yet trips on planes or commuter trains may provide the longest period of uninterrupted time a manager ever gets. During my years as a commuter to New York City, I experimented with how much work and what kind could be done effectively on the train. I found that there was a great inclination to go along with the majority and do nothing more than sleep or read the newspaper. But I discovered that when I was under pressure and put my mind to the task, I could get a great deal of work done if it was the right kind. On one occasion I answered 10 or 12 letters, several of them requiring careful attention and discussion of alternatives. On another occasion I wrote an article for publication, having previously given some thought to it and collected relevant materials.

DICTATING EQUIPMENT

Now we come to one of the most obvious tools at the disposal of the manager. The logic of using dictating equipment as a time saver is clear. It is designed to free the secretary for more important work while the exact words of the dictator are being faithfully recorded for her to retrieve later, at a time convenient for her. Every minute that the executive dictates into the mechanical device represents one minute saved for the secretary so that she can do other work.

Secretaries often resist the idea of dictating equipment. A feeling has evolved that the professional status of the secretary depends on her maintaining her stenographic skill. While she does need to do so, perhaps she also needs to understand that it is best used selectively. There are many more important things that she can do for her boss than sit there recording each of his words. Another reason secretaries may resist the idea of dictating equipment is that they dislike having to live through a possibly painful period of learning to use it well.

There also seems to be a reluctance on the part of many managers to attempt to use dictating equipment. Fear of an inability to use a mechanical device effectively may be compounded by an unwillingness to take the time necessary for mastering it. There may also be a reluctance to face the anticipated objections of the secretary.

A Daniel Howard survey shows that 40 percent of executives write letters and memos in longhand for their secretaries to type.[5] When you consider the agonizingly slow pace of handwriting—20 to 30 words per minute at best—compared with the speed of the spoken word—150 words a minute, the utility of dictating equipment becomes apparent. Moreover, a man can speak twice as fast as a secretary can take his words down in shorthand. Therefore one hour of dictating machine use is equal to at least five hours of the executive's time handwriting memos and letters or two hours of his time plus two of his secretary's giving and taking dictation.

An additional saving was brought to light by the U.S. Navy Management Office. It found that a secretary could transcribe from a machine 33 percent faster than from longhand or shorthand.

Clearly, dictating equipment is almost mandatory for managerial effectiveness. However, as with other tools, there may be some dangers inherent in its use. Talking into a machine can become so easy that letters and reports grow wordy and files bulge with unnecessary verbiage.

One of the newest concepts affecting office procedures and secretarial practices is known as "word processing." Originating in Germany, the concept calls for an analysis of the office workload to systematize and automate it for text preparation. Phrases used repetitively are "canned" so that they can be automatically typed when necessary. It is a process of having word originators such as executives, sales correspondents, and lawyers select formula clauses from precoded, preorganized clause books.

Secretarial time is freed from routine typing for more important administrative responsibilities, production is significantly increased, errors are reduced, and response time is speeded.

Jack Lutz, president of the Replacement Products Division of the McCord Corporation, finds the small, portable dictating device indispensable as a means of capturing the thoughts that flash through his mind as he drives to and from work and on trips. His dictating machine is a constant companion. Comparing it with the alternative of a note pad, he cites the danger that writing distracts one's attention from the road. He finds it relatively easy to pick up a dictating receiver and speak into it while keeping his eyes on the road. The value of capturing ideas when they are fresh has proved itself to him over and over again.

MEMOITIS

We are told that some 50 million file drawers hold an estimated 250 billion pieces of paper in American offices, and the total mounts daily. One estimate puts the paperwork cost of running this country's economy at a sum equal to one-seventh of the total yearly output of goods and services. It's not unlikely that a sizable slice of the paperwork mountain consists of memos.

Eric Webster, in his classic "Memo Mania," describes why memos are the bane of large corporations. In most of its forms, the memo is a survival from the industrial dark ages of quill pens, high stools, low-cost clerical staff, no telephones, and unlimited time. Full employment, says Webster, is a man and his memo pad.

Even the most famous names in industry are not immune to memoitis. In 1960, before a large oil company brought in management consultants, two tons of paper arrived daily at its head office. By 1966 the consultants had helped cut this to approximately one ton. Webster cites the cost of unnecessary memos as uncountable but colossal. This cost represents the time and effort spent on thinking through the intended message, dictating it, typing it, transmitting it, reading it, and disposing of it.

Webster divides the purposes of memos into various categories. There are those designed to postpone work (a note saying you are going to act enables you to do nothing for a little longer with a clear conscience); the memo to demonstrate efficiency (following my memo of the first of last month—I know what it says; let's see if you can find your copy); the militant memo (the missive from the mild little man who's afraid to come and say his piece); the accusative memo designed "for the record" (if the recipient does answer it—which will take hours—the sender can always contest the answers, and if he doesn't the memo man has him "fixed" in the files); the status-making memo (from the desk of—"The ultimate in idiocy is when you have two desks corresponding with each other"); and the see-how-hard-I'm-working memo (the insecure subordinate often showers memos on his boss's desk like confetti, and given half a chance he will spend more time telling what he's doing than doing it).

Most insidious of all, in Webster's opinion, is the blind-copy memo man, who writes ostensibly for one audience but is actually addressing the unseen, unlisted recipients of the blind copy. Each memo man develops his own in group and out group. The ins get everything. The outs get nothing and only hear the news of what they're supposed to be doing if a kindly in grouper lends them his copy of the memo. The effect is always better if the ins are the people who are not expected to react and the outs are those who actually do the work. Getting on the right lists can be like getting the key to the executive washroom. It's a real invitation to move with the mighty.[6]

Floods of irrelevant paper clog the arteries of the memo-bound organization. Frank Nunlist calls it "the paper blockade."

Nonetheless, a memo can serve a useful purpose in the hands of one who makes it his servant rather than his master. A simple rule: use it as seldom as possible. A memo is to remind, to clarify, to confirm. It may be better than a phone call when it is needed to sit on a desk and keep reminding or when it is sent to a lot of hard-to-locate people so that it actually saves telephoning time. But remember, it is one-way communication. On the phone you at least get a reaction. Person to person, you can read the response. Memo-bound institutions are usually fraught with misunderstandings and resentments. There is no quicker way for two executives to get out of touch with each other than to retire to the seclusion of their offices and start writing each other notes.

Memo control, like forms control, calls for an occasional inventory. Examine last month's output and input of memos. How many were unnecessary? How many could have been shorter? This will give you a measure of your own misdemeanors in memocraft and lead you to stop working in waste paper. In many cases managers find they do a better job just by doing the job rather than writing a memo about it.

Reading

The accelerating proliferation of knowledge has done much to complicate the manager's job in the last decade. For many in executive positions, the task of keeping up with relevant reading has simply grown out of bounds. As we saw in Chapter 3, some 83 percent of the chief executives responding to a Daniel Howard survey said they "did not have time to keep up with the reading in their field," [7] and they undoubtedly spoke for the overwhelming majority of American managers. Yet keeping up with developments in one's field can hardly be considered of secondary importance for managerial survival in the 1970s.

Not to know what is going on jeopardizes the future of any manager. Gerard O'Shea, proponent of "practiced reading," states:

> It is imperative to formulate a flexible system of selecting so that at least the daily information requirements are fulfilled. . . . New skills designed to aid priority selection and to increase understanding in varied material and reading rate flexibility are no longer nice things to have. Today they are necessities to service the basic needs of large organizations and corporations. [8]

Various approaches to the problem of keeping up with reading have been tried. Delegating reading assignments is one effective solution. The benefits of this practice include

1. Insuring that printed matter is immediately circulated to interested people.
2. Keeping your team informed of new developments in a timely way.
3. Requiring that the readers note the important items and possible applications, thus giving you the benefit of their thinking on new developments.
4. Giving you a measure of what is important to your men.
5. Taking the "reading monkey" off your back while insuring that essential reading will be accomplished because the responsibility has been placed on your team members.

SPEED READING

For the past two years in lectures and seminars on time management, I have queried the participants concerning their estimated time spent reading. A rough average of 30 percent is quickly agreed on by virtually every group. This means that the average manager will devote almost *one year* of the next three to reading! My next question: "How many of you have taken speed reading?" The responses will vary from 2 or 3 up to as many as 10 out of an average group of 50. Virtually all speed readers will have at least doubled their reading rate while increasing their comprehension. Most average a gain of between two and three times their former speed. So conservatively speaking a manager could, if he would, save six months of time in the next three years!

Generally, training in speed reading sets out to break down bad reading habits and introduce good new ones. For example,

1. Stop moving your head from side to side as you read each line.

2. Stop vocalizing by mouthing or speaking the words.

3. Stop rereading.

4. Increase your reading span—try to take in groups of words rather than single words each time your focus shifts.

5. Start with the second or third word of each line to stop wasting peripheral vision on margins.

The five-minute speed-reading test presented below was created by Hilda Yoder, of the Yoder School, New York City. Originally appearing in Carl Heyel's *Organizing Your Job in Management*,[9] the 500-word selection is of standard difficulty, the kind of material found in newspapers and general magazines. Before reading it note the time you start, and enter your finishing time at the end. Consult the accompanying table to find your reading speed.

Starting Time _____

Chances are good that you are stuffing your briefcase with more and more material to read at home. In virtually all middle- and top-level jobs, the flood of "required reading" has steadily increased.

Yet more businessmen could cut drastically—or even eliminate—the amount of such work they take home. The secret: developing more efficient reading habits.

Statistics show that most businessmen read below the college level—attaining only 300 words a minute or less—and that their comprehension of the material is far too low, and that 90 percent of them could at least double their reading speed and—much more important—boost their comprehension considerably.

To a slow reader, increasing speed and comprehension may seem impossible. He is likely to feel that the ability to read fast is a God-given talent possessed by only a favored few.

Actually, the rapid reader has received no such mystic blessing. The way a person reads is nothing more than a habit. And the slow, poor reader, by study and application, can usually become a good reader.

One way to change your reading habits is to go to a good clinic or teacher for a special course. This may well double or even triple the average executive's reading speed. One reason for this is the fact that methods for analyzing reading faults have been developed on a highly scientific plane. Here is just one example. The actual movements of your eye can be photographed, giving a graphic picture of such things as the number of fixations per line of type, backtracking, length of time to read a specific number of words.

But can you improve your reading skill on your own, without going to a professional source? Yes—if you are willing to study and practice. Just reading a book about how to improve your reading won't work, any more than just reading about exercise will strengthen your muscles.

Here are the broad principles involved. Authorities have found that most businessmen are likely to be perfectionists in reading. They read every word because they are afraid of missing something. Reading whole thoughts and phrases increases both speed and comprehension.

The best way to do this is by reading material of standard difficulty, such as most popular magazines or light novels. Time yourself, see how much you read in say ten minutes. Next day read the same length of time but try to read more text.

While doing this, concentrate on moving forward. Don't regress, or look back, trying to pick up something you missed. You will have trouble getting the full meaning at first, but the important thing here is to jostle yourself out of old reading habits.

One way to test your comprehension is to have someone ask you questions on what you have just read. A better way is to do this reading from books specifically designed to improve your skill. They include tests on comprehension that relate to their text.

Finishing Time _____

Minutes	*Words per minute*
5	100
4½	111
4	125
3½	143
3	166
2½	200
2	250
1½	333
1	500

To evaluate your comprehension of what you have just read, circle the answers to the following true-false questions about it. Answers are furnished in the notes.[10] Give yourself 10 points for each correct answer.

1. To cut his homework, a businessman needs to develop better reading habits. T _____ F _____

2. 99 percent of businessmen can improve their reading. T _____ F _____

3. Good reading is a maker of good habits. T _____ F _____

4. Reading habits can be analyzed. T _____ F _____

5. Reading techniques can be improved merely by knowing your difficulties. T _____ F _____

6. Perfectionists who must note every detail tend to be poor readers. T _____ F _____

7. Reading can be improved by looking for whole thoughts and phrases. T _____ F _____

8. The best way to improve reading is to choose for daily practice a book you find difficult to read. T _____ F _____

9. Looking back for a missed idea is a "must." T _____ F _____

10. Comprehension can be developed by reading books written for this purpose. T _____ F _____

Score	*Rating*
60 or lower	poor
70	passing
80	good
90	very good
100	excellent

This glance at the problem of slow reading and your own rating on speed and comprehension on the small test may prompt you to take action. If a reputable course in speed reading is not available at a nearby college or professional center, Carl Heyel's book will offer an excellent beginning.

An interesting variation on speed reading is "speed comprehension" training through "time-compressed speech." Sound tapes are played faster than they were recorded. Groups receiving practice material seven hours a day at 425 words per minute, which is 1½ times the normal speaking rate, have experienced an increase from a mean of 40 percent of normal speed comprehension on the first day to 70 percent on the fifth.[11]

SELECTIVE READING

"Would you like to be able to read 50,000 words a minute?" asks James McCay. "There are many times when it is easy to do this if you know how. All you have to be able to do is to recognize within one minute that a 50,000-word book does not suit your purposes, and decide *not* to read it!"[12] On the general subject of selectivity, we need say no more.

But McCay goes much farther. Most books and magazines have only a few ideas to offer that the reader can use at the time. The trick is to find those ideas as quickly as possible. If, as Gertrude Stein put it, a book has been a very true book for you, you will always read it again. McCay gives us three quick rules for selective reading:

1. Scan the table of contents for a rough picture of the book or magazine before exploring it.

2. Scan a book quickly—say for an hour or so—to get to know the author and how he talks. You cannot understand what a man means until you've listened to him for a while.

3. Read carefully the sections that look as though they contain information you are interested in.

Regarding selective reading, Frank Cochran, president of Bray Lines, says that when reading he always turns to the table of contents, determines the one or two pieces or chapters of real interest to him, and goes directly to them. He has found through experience that when he leafs through a magazine he inevitably becomes distracted by other interesting but irrelevant articles.

Chapter 5

Blocking

Interruptions

There is a subtle deceptiveness about interruptions. They are seldom recognized as such; they masquerade under a presumption of legitimacy.

Consider the in basket, for example. Is it not common for managers to assume that anything in their in baskets is there by right? This presumption of legitimacy may be the greatest single factor in preventing managers from routing items back to senders that should never have been sent in the first place.

Consider the legitimacy presumption attending telephone calls. How many managers accept phone calls in the middle of a conversation with another person in their office? How many salesmen leaving the office will stop because their phone rings? How many housewives have spent their lives answering telephone calls at supper time? It is incredible that people who would not think of bursting into an office and intruding on a personal conversation feel they can interrupt with impunity by calling from across the hall or down the street.

The presumption of legitimacy is also attached to the drop-in visitor. Who would come into our office without having good reason to do so? Even when it becomes patently evident that a visitor's sole purpose is to chat about last night's ball game, many managers still give him the benefit of the doubt.

There is of course a place for common courtesy. But courtesy need not extend carte blanche to calls or visits that destroy concentration and continuity of thought and effort. Such interruptions confuse priorities, create illusions of crisis, harm morale, and often create real crises by delaying needed information.

As George Berkwitt put it, "What gives the manager's job its nightmarish quality are the interruptions—the constant and seemingly endless telephone calls, sudden meetings and personnel problems that seem demonically designed to run his schedule off the track." [1]

While not all interruptions are necessarily time wasters, by definition it would seem that time wasters must often be interruptions. If something is wasting time, then something more important is not getting done.

Exhibit 9 shows the time wasters most often cited by managers. The location of the time waster identifies the managerial function with which it is most closely associated.

But identifying time wasters is not enough, as Sune Carlson learned from the managing directors he studied in Sweden.

The mere ascertainment that a particular behavior deviated from the given norm was, however, not enough. We had also to find out the reasons for such a deviation. A chief executive who is overworked, or who is overloaded by details, is not much helped by the information that all this is his own fault. If he does not understand the "pathological" process which has produced his present difficulties, and learn to notice the early symptoms of such a process, he may soon find himself in similar difficulties again. [2]

My experience leads me to agree with Carlson. In sessions with managers in which we attempt to develop solutions to

Exhibit 9. Time wasters related to management functions.

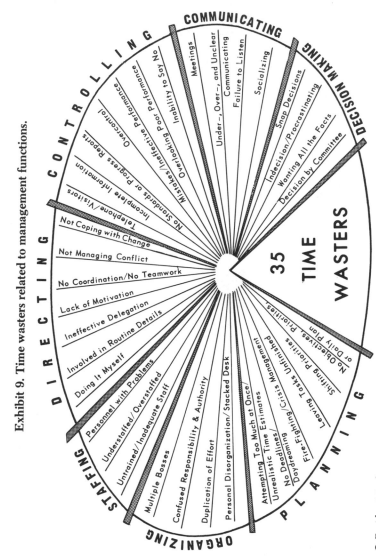

© R. Alec Mackenzie, 1972.

problems of time wasting, we invariably begin by inquiring into the probable causes of a time waster.

Visitors

Visitors cause problems for managers for a variety of reasons. One is the inherent difficulty of determining in advance what information one needs to know. As Curtis Symonds suggests, the information managers need *not* to know far exceeds in quantity the information that is essential.[3]

Not being able to foresee whether a visitor has an important communication leads to many open doors. Of course the nature of the manager's job may be such, as with the purchasing agent, that he depends on new information to be effective.

In addition to the need to keep informed, there are other forces at work that compound the visitor problem. Some of these are a penchant for socializing and a habit of procrastinating. The desire simply to know what's going on even outside the realm of one's work opens many doors to drop-in visitors.

We first observe that rules regarding the handling of telephones in offices are typically much more restrictive than those regarding visitors. Yet it is likely that more time is spent receiving visitors than on any other activity. The Sune Carlson study concluded that the chief executive's median time with visitors (mostly subordinates) was 3½ hours a day.

MANAGING VISITS

Let us begin our attack by listing the steps it is desirable to take *before* the visitor is allowed entrance.

Authorize your secretary to handle appointments This gives her the necessary authority to screen visitors also. If in doubt she should make tentative appointments subject to your approval.

Fix reception hours This is particularly necessary for the executive's staff. A fixed period, for example from 10:00 until

3:00, ought to be available for subordinates to schedule time with you simply by asking your secretary for the next available spot. They should be asked the purpose of the appointment and the length of time desired so that she can advise you and prepare any necessary papers.

Have visitors screened   The secretary's desk ought to be positioned so that no passerby can drop in without being intercepted. The secretary should be trained in courteous interception procedures. A simple "May I help you?" in a friendly voice will generally suffice. She should answer the question "Is he busy?" with "Yes, he is at the moment. Could he call you?" or "Would you like me to interrupt him?" This action often prevents an interruption. After all, the drop-in visitor does not have an appointment and is not automatically entitled to the presumption that his matter is more important than whatever work the executive happens to be doing.

Go to the subordinate's office   When a staff member asks whether he may drop in for a few minutes, answer by asking the urgency of the matter. If it is not an emergency, then ask, "Can it wait 10 minutes? I'll drop by." A Dutch managing director in Holland listed these advantages of such a procedure: (1) It avoids an interruption and allows you to finish the matter at hand before seeing the subordinate. (2) By preventing his coming to sit down by your desk, you do not lose control of your own office. (3) By going to his office, you maintain control of the situation because you can leave at any time. (4) You are nearer the problem—the files, the blueprint, whatever the question involves. (5) You pay him a compliment by going to him.

Meet the visitor outside your office   If a visitor does not announce his purpose, do not invite him into your office, where you lose control. Go to see him in the outer office or in the lobby. Give him a friendly handshake and a warm inquiry, "Can I help you?" to determine the reason for the call immediately. Meeting the visitor outside your office makes it much easier to limit the duration of the call.

Confer standing up   When a visitor pops in either because the secretary missed the interception or he refused to recognize it, stand up. With a friendly greeting quickly determine the priority—decide whether to allow the interruption or to defer it to another time. By standing up you prevent the visitor from sitting down, thereby gaining psychological control.

Have your secretary monitor the visit The secretary should know the purpose of all calls. Using her own good judgment based on prior discussions with you, after the passage of a reasonable amount of time, she should either telephone you or open the door to remind you of an obligation that must be attended to. This gives you the opportunity to bring the visit to a timely close or to respond to the secretary, "We'll be through in five minutes," which alerts not only her but also the visitor to your intentions.

Time-limit the visit Make a forthright statement at the outset of how much time you have available. When visits by subordinates are arranged by telephone, the time-limiting is a matter for the secretary to attend to and should pose little problem.

Block interruptions Allow no calls or interruptions of any kind except for extreme emergencies. The one exception is the monitoring call from the secretary.

Meet regularly When Charles Percy was president of Bell & Howell Company, he had lunch with a different associate every day as a means of keeping informed and discussing matters of mutual interest. Such a practice with individual people or with your team can do much to minimize the need for the drop-in visit or even scheduled meetings. The principal purpose of many executive dining rooms is to provide the opportunity for the top executives to meet on a regular, informal basis while saving the time required to go out for lunch.

CLOSING THE OPEN DOOR

It is a myth that the open-door policy always improves managerial effectiveness. In fact, it can destroy the manager's effectiveness if it is used poorly. How this policy got started is not difficult to understand. With the move toward people-oriented management, the argument that bosses were hard to get to made sense; a hallway with all the doors closed could promote a sense of exclusion. To demonstrate that bosses could be seen at any time, many companies overreacted by adopting the open-door policy.

Yet being always available is no guarantee of success as a manager. On the contrary, it may encourage dependence and serve as an invitation to interruptions that will fragment the manager's day. It may also result in the upward delegation of decisions, forcing him to work below his level and involving him in details that take time away from more important matters.

Perhaps the worst thing about the open door is the inflexibility it implies. Responsiveness to changing situations, the varying needs of subordinates, and the shifting priorities of the job ought to suggest freedom in such matters as keeping one's office door open or closed. The key is not the door but the manager and how he handles the situation.

As Don Mitchell says, "A manager with many daily problems and 'fire drills' simply cannot spend the time he needs to think intelligently about the future unless he can isolate himself for a while." [4] He *must* have time without interruptions.

He may use various methods to obtain this time. Two have already been discussed: taking a quiet hour at the beginning of the day's work and establishing visiting hours for subordinates.

A third method is to come to the office early. Staying late unfortunately is often unprofitable. Too many people are "unencumbered" for the evening and will drop by just to kill time. Early arrival is another story. Nobody else is there without a serious purpose.

A fourth method is to have a hideaway—a separate office, a special room, another man's office. Not only are there fewer interruptions (only your secretary knows where you are) but the atmosphere is different; there is a relaxation in different surroundings. A management professor reports getting a great deal of work done in a hideaway office where he spends afternoons, separated from his regular public-seeing office. Many companies provide a "quiet room" or library executives may use. Economics Laboratory has a travel hideaway: this is a hotel room where a manager returning from an absence and needing seclusion can catch up on his work.

W. E. Uzzell, president of Royal Crown Cola Company, says, "The office is a fine place for day-to-day activities. But it's not the best place for big thinking. Even when the door is closed, I always have the feeling that something I should know about is going on outside at the secretary's desk. . . . My favorite thinking spot is a cottage at a nearby lake."

Charles Hummel, president of Barrington College, makes such trips a regular part of his schedule. He spends one day a month in a hideaway where he plans the following month's activities.

It is interesting to note the ease with which a manager will plan and succeed in taking a trip out of town. He makes arrangements and gets himself en route at the required hour. Somehow it seems to take double the effort to say, "Tomorrow morning at 9:00 I am going to be in an unidentified office and remain for the day or until the job is done."

SOCIALIZING

The drop-in visitor, aided and abetted by the open door, is but part of an all-encompassing time waster we could identify as "socializing." This monumental distracter occurs when drop-in visitors arrive, when people with scheduled appointments are encouraged to warm up to their subject by telling you about their vacation, when telephone calls are prolonged unnecessarily, or when meetings start late or veer off the subject.

The practice also creeps insidiously into correspondence and memos. The "friendly note" first tells how your family is doing and where the last vacation was before getting to the purpose of the missive, and then it goes on to ask how the recipient's family is. Social creatures that we are, the tendency to socialize is universal. The effective manager must maintain an unceasing vigil against it.

A group of executives completing a seminar on time man-

agement listed certain items they intended to act on after returning to their jobs. Included in their list was, "Learn how
to terminate conversations."

The Telephone

The telephone is of course one of the greatest time savers.
There are many ways in which judicious use of this instrument saves time.

1. It saves a meeting and the time involved in getting to it
by bridging the distance between parties.

2. It saves multiple calls. A conference call brings many
people together and thus saves enormous aggregate travel
time. Multicountry and even multicontinent conference calls
are common. (As many as 49 separate locations can be connected in one telephone conference.) Once a month the 750
top officers of the United States Postal Service meet in their
15 regional offices across the country and in their Washington
headquarters. On the day following the monthly staff meeting
in Washington, where operational problems and programs
are discussed and programs finalized, all 15 regional offices,
with 50 or 60 staff people in each, are connected by wire in a
telephone conference. They learn—and learn immediately—
what has happened the previous month and what new programs are being activated.

3. It saves useless trips. Many salesmen have spared themselves a trip by calling ahead and finding that the prospect
will not be in his office. Managers who wisely phone to recon-
firm an appointment save fruitless travel if the date can't be
kept.

4. It saves letters and the waiting they entail. Given the
time it takes to consider, dictate, type, proof, sign, and deliver
a letter, and the possibility that the intended recipient may be
delayed getting to it, a phone call making virtually instanta-
neous contact may cost less and do the job better. In this
connection the advantage of the telephone becomes even
greater—it offers two-way communication. If discussion is
called for, the matter can be settled on the spot.

In New York City as many as 38 million telephone calls and in the country as·many as 480 million have been made in a single day. One can imagine the amount of communication which transpires in the course of all of these calls and the amount of saved travel time represented.

THE CAUSES OF TELEPHONE SLAVERY

Ironically the telephone, one of the most effective time savers, is also one of the biggest time wasters. How does this instrument of efficiency get out of hand? How does it happen that many managers allow themselves to become slaves of the telephone rather than its master?

Among the more obvious reasons is an executive's desire to be involved in everything. A certain lack of self-discipline enters into this situation also. An inability to terminate conversations and a fear of offending people by having calls screened are frequently at fault. Perhaps those who suffer most from this affliction are managers who have never learned to use secretaries effectively.

Nine out of ten executives spend at least an hour each day on the phone and four out of ten spend more than two hours per day, so the urgent need for telephone discipline is evident. A devastating factor in the battle for control over our environment is the incoming call. On this tactical battlefield lie the shattered nerves of many a manager who conquered other, more imposing time robbers. Executives with secretarial help head inexorably down the road to defeat when they fail to give their secretaries authority in this critical area.

INCOMING CALLS

In the interests of sound management, our objective is to prevent incoming calls from destroying the manager's concentration. This goal calls for professional intercession by a skilled secretary.

Her first purpose as she receives the call should be to determine the urgency of the matter and the appropriate party to handle it. Managers who set out to master their time almost always discover that a great number of incoming calls in fact are misdirected. Others in their organization can provide the required information faster and better. These are the easy calls. More difficult is the call on a subject that is within the manager's area of responsibility but that his secretary or others can deal with. In a diplomatic way she must discover the purpose of the call and ask whether she may provide that information since she has it at hand.

Another kind of call concerns questions that only the manager can handle but that are not of sufficient urgency to warrant his being interrupted. "May he call you back when he is free?" is an appropriate inquiry for the secretary to make. Many managers prefer the automatic call-back response for everything but emergencies. This is a strong and highly effective position. It implies that the manager is indeed busy and that he ought to continue uninterrupted until he can return calls at a moment convenient for himself.

While it is true that the timing of the return call may not be convenient to the original phoner, it is a simple matter of balancing the equities. Why should his purpose in calling be automatically presumed more important than the manager's purpose in completing his current task?

The talented secretary can develop the art of being helpful to both parties in this situation. Putting the caller on hold with a simple "Let me see if I can interrupt him," she asks the manager for a brief response that will suffice for the caller. This type of interruption may be so fast and so easily handled that it does not destroy the manager's continuity. He immediately resumes his task while the secretary provides the requested information to the caller. This degree of collaboration between secretary and manager comes only from practice. It takes a long time to work out but is invaluable for ultimate effectiveness.

Then there is the urgent call, predesignated by the manager as having a priority that warrants immediate interruption. Bosses who are sensitive to their subordinates' time set up procedures to guard against what has been termed an "up-grading of calls" from the boss. The secretary who says merely, "Mr. Cooper is calling for Mr. Smith," forces Mr. Smith's secretary to interrupt his meeting to say that the boss wants him. This leaves Mr. Smith with little alternative but to take the call regardless of its importance. A more aware boss—or secretary—will anticipate this "upgrading" danger and make sure that an unpressing matter is simply conveyed by message through Mr. Smith's secretary for response at a time convenient to him.

How does the secretary handle the telephone inquiry that she thinks but is not certain is important enough to bring to her boss's attention? Perhaps her best procedure is to say, "He's busy at the moment. Would you like me to interrupt him?" This puts the decision on relative urgency squarely back with the caller. It generally works very well, particularly for the secretary who asks the question in a very helpful and friendly tone of voice so that it is clear she would like to help the caller if she can.

The call-back system The tremendous advantages of the call-back system deserve amplification. The executive who is making full use of this technique will determine in advance when he wishes to return calls. He may choose two times— for example, one late in the morning and the other late in the afternoon—when he is likely to find the other party facing lunch engagements or quitting time and less likely to wish to socialize.

The grouping of calls in this fashion reduces the number of interruptions dramatically. It places them at a moment convenient to the manager, not the caller. It allows time for the caller to solve his problem another way. (Some people, when asked whether the manager may phone back at 11:00, will respond, "Well, no, I guess not. I'll find the answer another way.") The call-back system also permits the secretary to have the required information at the executive's hand when he phones, which shortens the time required and allows him time to consider his response or to get other opinions.

The objection most managers have to using this system is

the fear that a caller will be offended by being screened. However, if the secretary assures him of a return call *before* she asks for his name, this will prevent him from feeling he is being screened out.

In support of the call-back method, Joseph Trickett observed:

> No one expects a physician or surgeon to answer the phone during an examination or operation. No jurist is expected to answer the phone while he is in court. No professor is expected to answer his phone while he is teaching a class. Why, then, should an important business executive be expected to be always "on tap" and available to his telephone? [5]

OUTGOING CALLS

Don't dial your own Despite what some managers say, it's generally a mistake to place your own outgoing calls when a secretary is available to do so. Surprisingly, most executives have their secretaries place their local calls only rarely. Yet the manager who does his own phoning is extremely likely to waste his time failing to get through or reaching the other man's secretary only to be told that the intended recipient is out. The cost of this method is clearly prohibitive.

Robert Townsend is quoted as saying, and in fact has permitted his picture to appear in a full-page telephone company ad announcing, that he makes a practice of placing his own long-distance calls. While the point of the ad was that direct calls station to station are cheaper than operator-assisted calls person to person, Townsend also emphasizes that it's he—not his secretary—who puts them in: "I've long believed in dialing my own long-distance calls. For one thing, it gives me a chance to get 'up' for my dialogue. For another thing, it's usually faster, and it saves me money, too." [6]

Faster? Maybe if he's lucky enough to catch his man. Cheaper? How much does he figure his time is worth when he's playing switchboard operator?

Peter Drucker makes some tongue-in-cheek remarks about Townsend's telephone practices:

Since I practice many of the things that Townsend preaches, I am, of course, very much on his side. I have, for instance, always answered my own telephone. But I always suspected that I did so because I am incurably nosy, don't delegate anyhow, and find that chatting on the telephone beats working by a long shot. I'm therefore delighted to be told by Townsend that my old bad habits are executive virtues.[7]

Not only should outgoing calls be placed by secretaries but they ought to be grouped. Select a good time of day, and make as many of your calls as you can together. Have your material handy and your subject outlined. Failure to jot down the points to be covered often leads to oversights. How many times have you hung up just before remembering that other point you wanted to ask about?

As a courtesy, says one executive, refrain from asking, "Are you busy?" The response will usually be courteously negative —but often false. Rather ask, "Are you in a meeting?" A direct question like this will draw a direct response. If he is, give a terse message or ask him to call you back when free.

CURTAIL YOUR CALLS

Most experienced executives agree that the opening dictates the ending of telephone conversations. "Hi, Joe. How are you?" is an invitation to a long conversation including current events, family life, golf, vacation, and so forth. Conversely, "Hi, Joe. I need a couple of quick answers if you have a minute" will guarantee a short phone call and perhaps relieve the other fellow that he doesn't have to waste his time socializing either. Also learn how to terminate conversations. How many telephone visits have dragged on endlessly because both visitors lacked terminating facilities? Try, "Fine, Bill. Hope this helps. See you at Rotary." Consider the telephone as a message machine and get off the line promptly.

An innovative method, mentioned at the beginning of the book, was applied by an executive who received a call at a particularly inopportune moment. He simply hung up in midconversation—while *he* was talking! End of conversation.

Sometimes it takes imagination to discourage the frequent telephoner. There is the story of the supervisor whose subordinate was in the habit of calling him up to ask him for decisions on the most minor items. The manager decided to put an end to the practice. The man called and inquired, "Boss, I'm halfway through taking the inventory, but the last shipment of lumber came for completing the addition to the crib. Should I complete the inventory or stop that and finish the addition to the crib?"

The manager paused for a moment, said, "Yes," and hung up. A moment later his phone rang again. It was the subordinate, asking in a puzzled voice, "Boss, did you mean, yes, finish the inventory, or yes, finish the addition to the crib?" The boss again paused, said, "No," and hung up.

Meetings

Ask any group of managers in any country in the world to list their three most time-consuming activities. Give them a few moments to reflect and discuss the question. Invariably "meetings" will appear among the three. I have asked this question of more than 200 groups, and in every case but 3, more than three-fourths of each group indicated that *half their time spent in meetings is wasted.* The problem, lamented a friend of mine, is in not being sure which half.

Since surveys indicate that some middle managers spend up to 80 percent of their time in meetings, the seriousness of this finding is evident.

One experienced executive said, "The biggest waste of time in our company is our top management meeting on Monday mornings. We don't know where we are going or why, so we never know when we arrive. We do know it is Monday and we always meet on Monday. What I can't stand is an aimless, meandering meeting." [8]

WHY, WHO, WHEN, AND WHERE

First and perhaps most commonly, meetings are called for purposes of coordinating activities, exchanging information, and building morale. Second is the participative, problem-solving, decision-formulating meeting. An offshoot of this might be designated the risk-sharing meeting, convened for the sometimes hidden purpose of sharing the risk of an unpopular, chancy, or difficult decision.

Many meetings should not occur at all. Among them are those a manager calls because he is unable or unwilling to make a decision. Another inappropriate reason is a compulsion toward overcommunication; these are meetings for the sake of meetings. Salute the leader who calls a meeting for information and coordination purposes, asks at the end whether anyone has anything of importance to add, and when the response is negative immediately adjourns the meeting with "Well, then, let's get back to work."

Having disposed of meetings that should never have been called, we turn to meetings that, though necessary, are poorly prepared. For example, take the one whose purpose has not been defined. "Let's get together and talk it over," says the manager. Second thought might well have showed him that the function of the meeting was not yet clear enough in his own mind to warrant calling the team together. Or a meeting may accomplish little because critical information is lacking or because an agenda has not been set.

A meeting may bog down also if the manager neglects to consider who the essential people are and, even more important, who the unnecessary ones are, participants whose time will be wasted. The desire to appear to be democratic or not to slight anyone comes into play here. Hensleigh Wedgwood portrays the direct relationship between the number of people involved in a committee meeting and the confusion resulting from the increase in channels of communication:

> Why is it that group meetings are so often ineffectual in solving problems? There are many reasons, both practical and psychological. The first and most obvious is simply that the larger the group, the greater the difficulty in establishing communication among the individuals in it. In a "group" of two, communication is comparatively easy, because there are only two communication channels. But add a third person to this group and you immediately set up

six channels. Add a fourth and you have twelve; get eight people together and you have 56 channels to sort out and so on.

It follows that the larger the size of the group, the less likelihood there is of utilizing fully the resources of its individual members and the less control the Chairman will be able to exercise in bringing the meeting to a consensus or any resolution of the problems it has set out to solve.[9]

An innovative approach to the monumental problem of meetings was taken by administrators in the Greenwich, Connecticut, school system. They decided to attack the trouble at its source—the existence of committees. They took inventory of all the committees in the system, asking critical questions about the purpose of each and the extent to which that purpose had been achieved. As a result more than 50 committees were identified, and of these more than 20 were abolished. Think back for a moment to the committees you have known where the members, having completed their mission, sit back and say, "Now, that's done. What's next?" The Greenwich school administrators have really made it quite easy. Why should a committee that doesn't exist want to meet at all? Termination of a committee should be decided by date or by completion of function when the committee is established.

Consider also the bad timing of many committee meetings. For example, it is poor judgment to call one for a' time when certain key people will not be available. There is also a time of day that may be far the best. A meeting scheduled for a time when no other important events will require the attendance of any of its members until considerably later will be susceptible to running over. Meetings strategically set a half-hour or an hour before lunch or quitting time will more likely end on time. The participants' eye on the clock can greatly help the chairman keep the meeting on the track and dispense with extraneous though interesting side ventures. But external restraints alone will not suffice. Intelligent, aware, and objective-oriented leadership is required for meetings to succeed.

Finally, the selection of a poor location and the failure to anticipate equipment needs are common failings in preparing for meetings. Physical facilities that are not conducive to concentration because of noise, lack of ventilation, or other drawbacks are a bad choice. Likewise, locating a meeting too far from the majority of participants or where needed display or visual equipment is not available is also a mistake.

THE HIGH COST OF MEETINGS

In a seminar for 20 top managers, the meeting started 30 minutes late. On a rough estimate of the average salary of these executives, not including fringes, plus a few other expenses, that meeting cost nearly $500 before it got underway. Of course this made for a beautiful introduction. We began with the high cost of meetings!

Following a seminar on time management, a group of educational administrators in a large city school system calculated the cost of meeting. When their full staff was in attendance, the cost came to $50 per minute. No wonder the Econometer was designed by a Danish firm. Its announced purpose: to cut down on management meeting addiction by computing the total cost minute by minute on the basis of the number of participants and their average annual salary. Installed in a conference room, it operates like an electricity meter: the higher the power consumption, the faster the disk rotates and the higher the bill. The scoreboard covers meeting costs up to $9,999. Some meetings, explains the manufacturer, cost three times as much as savings gained through decisions made at them.

Perhaps this was what Ira Gottfried had in mind when he proposed a cost-to-benefit ratio analysis of meetings. Consider, he suggested, the labor costs in preparation, salaries of the attendees, overhead and fringe costs, travel expense, and lost time before, during, and after the meeting. Before planning that meeting, he concludes, make sure that the benefits to be expected are at least equal to the costs.[10]

DISCOURAGE TIME OVERRUNS

Failure to time-limit a meeting is an invitation to inflated costs. Without the prod of a deadline, participants often wax verbose. To paraphrase Parkinson, words expand to fill the time available.

Many managers feel that one hour ought to be sufficient for all but exceptionally important meetings. Some executives, when first imposing a time limit, have been sensitive to what they anticipated would be the reaction. However, those who persevere and end the discussion at the appointed time discover that participants very quickly adjust. At subsequent meetings decisions are arrived at faster. Furthermore, those present can plan their time following the meeting with more certainty.

Any meeting that lasts too long is allowed to. Take the traditional half- or full-day staff or executive committee conferences, research and development sessions, and so forth. The ease with which a set routine can be established is astonishing. I asked one executive who chaired periodic day-long meetings why they lasted so long. He responded, "I don't know. I guess they always have."

One reason conventional meetings last too long is that people unconsciously postpone the exertion of rising from a comfortable chair. As a result, conversations drag on into repetition and unnecessary excursions down blind alleys. The Steelcraft Mfg. Company discovered a corrective by chance in the "stand-up meeting." This format was born of repeated incidents. Executives found themselves meeting in halls, talking over problems on the run. When the subject was confidential, two or three of them usually wound up in a private office, finishing the discussion on their feet.

They soon found these stand-up meetings paying off handsomely. They did not get involved in too much detail concerning a problem or project. And they reached decisions faster. Of course, if anyone was dissatisfied with a decision too hastily arrived at or ill-considered, he was free to reactivate the matter at a regular meeting.

In fact, quick stand-up meetings have been used the day before scheduled meetings as thought starters. Presenting a problem in advance gives people a chance to mull it over, to sleep on it, so that they may be able to come to the formal meeting better prepared, their minds stimulated and ready for serious consideration and decision making.

One group proposed that a clock showing "minutes remaining" be placed on the wall of the meeting room. Every glance at the clock would be a stern reminder that time was passing.

Another, more humorous solution is provided by one executive who claims to have had two inches cut off the front legs of his conference room chairs. This, he asserts, has shortened meetings considerably.

ROLES PEOPLE PLAY IN MEETINGS

In Wedgwood's insightful analysis of committees, he describes in outline form the roles members play. Because of the direct correlation between the activities cited and time wasted and conserved, this outline is presented below.

GROUP-BLOCKING ROLES

The aggressor	Criticizes and deflates status of others; disagrees with others aggressively.
The blocker	Stubbornly disagrees; rejects others' views; cites unrelated personal experiences; returns to topics already resolved.
The withdrawer	Won't participate; "wool gatherer"; converses privately; self-appointed note-taker.
The recognition seeker	Boasts; excessive talking; conscious of his status.
The topic jumper	Continually changes subject.
The dominator	Tries to take over, assert authority, manipulate group.
The special-interest pleader	Uses group's time to plead his own case.
The playboy	Wastes group's time showing off; story teller; nonchalant; cynical.
The self-confessor	Talks irrelevantly about his own feelings and insights.
The devil's advocate	More devil than advocate.

Group-Building Roles

The initiator	Suggests new or different ideas for discussion and approaches to problems.
The opinion giver	States pertinent beliefs about discussion and others' suggestions.
The elaborator	Builds on suggestions of others.
The clarifier	Gives relevant examples; offers rationales; probes for meaning and understanding; restates problems.
The tester	Raises questions to "test out" whether group is ready to come to a decision.
The summarizer	Reviews discussion; pulls it together.

Group Maintenance Roles

The tension reliever	Uses humor or calls for break at appropriate times to draw off negative feelings.
The compromiser	Willing to yield when necessary for progress.
The harmonizer	Mediates differences; reconciles points of view.
The encourager	Praises and supports others; friendly; encouraging.
The gate keeper	Keeps communications open; encourages participation.[11]

This outline focuses the spotlight on the critical role of the leader. The leader must of course be sensitive to the needs and feelings of the participants and flexible enough to adapt his style to meet each situation that arises. He should also have the ability, according to Wedgwood, to encourage each participant to assume roles that will help rather than hinder the group in coming to a decision or in reaching its goal.

Antony Jay gives us insight into one of the forces that often makes people refuse to play any productive role in a meeting:

I once attended a meeting called by the chairman of an engineering corporation to which all the heads of the operating companies were summoned. . . . There, around the table, were the eight or nine people who between them carried the top-line authority of the whole group. . . . Any poker player would have recognized the atmosphere at once. Cards were being played very close to the vest; remarks were studiously noncommittal, and clearly framed for their effect on the others—especially the chairman. The only subjects which relieved the taciturn caution of this meeting were the trivial ones, when suddenly everyone seemed to have a great deal to contribute. . . . It would all have been very puzzling to me as an observer, if I had not at other meetings and as a participant behaved in exactly the same way myself.

My meetings were at a much less exalted level, back in the days when I, as head of a department, met with other department heads, but my motives were the same. I knew that my department's interests and my own ego were better served by keeping quiet about facts, figures, and intentions which might not meet with approval, or which might provoke the other departmental heads to outcry or rivalry or proof of their superior awareness or achievement. I would happily talk about unimportant subjects or general principles of policy, but my department's operations were my own business.[12]

The hidden forces at work in such meetings obviously require sensitive and skillful leadership. To understand the roles people are playing requires real perception.

STARTING ON TIME

Specific time wasters that are operative during a meeting begin with the failure to start it on time. This is an annoyance often grumbled about but seldom corrected. It would seem fairly obvious that this is one time waster something *could* be done about. What's so difficult about doing what you say you will do? Launch the discussion when it is set to begin!

Directors of meetings who habitually start them from 15 minutes to 30 minutes late have asked me, "But how do you get people to get here on time?" My answer is always the same: "By starting on time." As long as the leader allows the practices of the least disciplined to dictate the practices of the group, the proceedings will *never* start on time. Of course there will be some who will be late to the first meeting he begins on schedule. Maybe a few will be late twice. Those who are late three times will (1) be in the small minority, (2) be telling you something about their interest in the meeting, or (3) be giving you a new perspective on how much they are really needed. Every way you come out ahead. But most of all you are being fair to those who care enough about the subject and respect other people's time enough to arrive on time. I know of a meeting that was called on time, started on time, and ended 10 minutes later with several critical decisions made that affected areas of absentee executives' responsibilities.

Charles E. Wilson, head of General Electric and famed for his mobilization of American industry in World War II, was also known as a record setter for brief meetings. He would hold 5- to 10-minute conferences in which he hastened to the point, reached a decision, and adjourned the meeting.[13]

GETTING AND STICKING TO THE POINT

Not only are many meetings late starting; many are also painfully slow getting to the point. This, of course, is a matter of meeting leadership.

"Before we start the meeting, Joe," says a chairman in a typical prestartup effort to get one small point out of the way —often while keeping an assembled group waiting. Also it is not always easy to identify the point of a meeting. Problem analysis may be needed to determine first whether a problem really exists. How often do we call a meeting just to decide whether we ought to be meeting?

The meeting that settles quickly down to business will nonetheless waste its participants' time if the discussion deviates from the agenda. The "meandering meeting" is one of the most common causes of complaints reflecting weak leadership. The chairman who allows a topic jumper to change the subject or, worse, who himself leads the discussion astray is performing a great disservice to the intended purpose of the meeting and to those he has asked to attend it. While some chairmen may argue that the wandering is "necessary to allow participation," this is rationalization. Participation that is meaningless, destroys continuity, and inhibits the accomplishment of the stated mission of the meeting is not the kind of involvement that should be sought.

It has been proposed that deviations from the agenda are often caused by failure to listen. The participant who is not paying attention is far more likely to give voice to a random thought triggered by an isolated phrase than is someone whose mind is on the proceedings. Needless to say, every executive should be considering carefully what contributions he can make if any and attempting to fulfill a group-building or group-maintaining role. Ralph Nichols, who pioneered in studying the listening side of communication at the University of Minnesota, first pointed out the tendency of people to be so intent on what they are going to say that they fail to listen to what is being said.

One executive decided on a radical innovation to prevent constant deviations from the agenda. He got tired of participants' "shooting from the lip" and inaugurated what he called a "psychological minute," a self-imposed silence following the presentation of a serious question or major problem. It insured that the first person beginning to talk did so after having time to think. It reduced extraneous comments and irrelevant discussion. It encouraged listening rather than speaking.

TIME-LIMITING THE AGENDA

Parkinson's Second Law states that we tend to devote time and effort to tasks in inverse relation to their importance. This principle is seen in action in many business meetings.

Chairmen may wish to time-limit the subjects on the agenda as a means of insuring that the time devoted to each will be in accordance with its relative importance. The pastor of a church in a suburb of Chicago was describing a case in point. At a meeting of the board of trustees called to make the final decision on a $350,000 budget, someone brought up the quality of the paper towels used in the kitchen and the rest rooms. The discussion that ensued had gone on approximately 35 minutes when one of the trustees, who had other things to do that evening, looked at his watch and expressed the hope that they could get to the principal item of business before he had to leave. With this reminder of the passage of time, the board members moved to the matter of the budget, discussed it for 15 minutes, and voted final approval. While the budget had been under previous consideration, the pastor chuckled as he recounted this story of how relative priorities get distorted in meetings. The paper towels had taken up more than twice as much time as the annual budget.

A medical center director with 20 doctors on his board of directors told me an interesting experience of a decision regarding a huge tree, located directly in front of the center, that had split in a storm and was now endangering the building. The decision involved whether to have the tree taken down or to cable it for safety. The doctors, who were used to making many important decisions for the center, met three times to discuss the future of the tree. Finally they decided that none of them knew that much about handling large trees, so they agreed to call in an expert. The salaries of the 20 doctors, prorated over the decision time spent on the tree, exceeded the total cost of the tree removal.

A time profile of a meeting is a recording of the number of minutes spent discussing each item on an agenda compared with a rating of the relative importance of the item. This is usually very revealing of how time is misapplied with respect to priorities on the agenda.

ENDING ON TIME

If we could cite as an axiom "Start late—end late," then the way to end meetings on time is to begin them on time. Just as I suggested that meetings will not start on schedule until the leader forces the issue, so with ending—none will end on time until he learns to lower the boom.

The principal resistance to ending on time predictably comes from the person most interested in the items remaining to be discussed. The sensitive leader at this point simply suggests alternatives. "If it can't wait until our next meeting, Bill, would you and Charlie like to come into my office to settle it now?" As soon as participants see that a chairman is serious about finishing according to schedule, they will begin disciplining themselves to get the agenda covered in the designated time.

If ending on time becomes a fetish, one may sacrifice valuable discussion and new ideas for the sake of a few minutes. This could of course be false economy. Judgment must be exercised in such cases.

SUMMARIZING

Meeting leaders commonly neglect to summarize progress or decisions made before adjourning. Such a summary focuses attention on the most critical elements of the meeting—what decisions were made or what goals reached. Everyone who leaves a meeting should feel something has been accomplished.

Perhaps the most glaring time waster in the postmeeting phase is the failure to prepare concise minutes that record the actions taken. Although often viewed as a time-consuming requirement, well-written minutes disseminated as soon as possible after meetings prevent misunderstandings and save time in followup.

Next to no minutes, perhaps the most serious postmeeting time waster is poor minutes. Fuzzy, imprecise notes that attempt to review impressions of discussions are difficult to write, time-consuming to read, and often of little value. After some experience with minutes, the chairman may want to instruct the preparer to leave out reports of discussions and to concentrate on decisions made, responsibilities assigned for followup, and deadlines for action to be taken. Thus the minutes become a tool for the precise delegation of responsibility. A simple form merely lists the identity of the group that met, the date, and those attending at the top of a sheet. Below this comes information summarizing the salient accomplishments in three columns headed "Responsibility" (who is to handle each matter), "Decisions," and "Deadlines."

A final postmeeting time waster is the failure to follow up. Decisions that are taken are dutifully recorded with responsibility for execution clearly stated. Yet because managers are wont to become harried by the pressure of events, to let things pile up, and to manage by chance rather than plan, the duties of following up previous decisions often remain undone. All the more reason for reducing this chore to a routine procedure. A way to do this is to make the uncompleted assignments recorded in the minutes the first items on the agenda for the next meeting, under the heading "Unfinished business." Such an automatic followup procedure is indispensable for insuring that decisions are executed.

TWENTY-ONE RULES FOR GETTING MORE FROM MEETINGS

In summary, 21 suggestions for limiting the time wasted in meetings are listed below. They are separated into categories pertaining to before, during, and after the meeting takes place.

BEFORE

1. Explore alternatives to meeting.
   a. A decision by the responsible party often eliminates the need for group action.
   b. A conference call may substitute for getting together.
   c. Postpone the meeting. Consolidate the agenda with that of a later meeting.
   d. Cancel the meeting. Ask yourself, "Is this meeting necessary?"
   e. Send a representative. This gives a subordinate experience and saves your time.
2. Limit your attendance. Attend only for the time needed to make your contribution.
3. Keep the participants to a minimum. Only those needed should attend.

4. Choose an appropriate time. The necessary facts and people should be available. Schedule the meeting for before lunch, another engagement, or quitting time if this is appropriate to the type of meeting being called.
5. Choose an appropriate place. Accessibility of location, availability of equipment, size of the room, and so forth are all important.
6. Define the purpose clearly in your own mind before calling the meeting.
7. Distribute the agenda in advance. This helps the participants prepare—or at least forewarns them.
8. Compute the cost per minute of meeting by figuring the total salaries per minute, adding perhaps 35 percent for fringes. Assess the cost of starting late and of the time allocated to the topics on the agenda.
9. Time-limit the meeting and the agenda. Allocate a time to each subject proportional to its relative importance.

During

10. Start on time. Give warning; then do it. There is no substitute.
11. Assign timekeeping and minutes responsibilities. Keep posted on the time remaining and the amount behind schedule if any.
12. Hold a stand-up meeting if appropriate. This speeds deliberations. Try it on drop-in visitors.
13. Start with and stick to the agenda. "We're here to. . . . The purpose of this meeting is. . . . The next point to be decided is. . . ."
14. Control interruptions. Allow interruptions for emergency purposes only.
15. Accomplish your purpose. What was the specific purpose of the meeting—to analyze a problem, to generate creative alternatives, to arrive at a decision, to inform, to coordinate? *Was it accomplished?*
16. Restate conclusions and assignments to insure agreement and to provide reinforcement or a reminder.
17. End on time. Adjourn the meeting as scheduled so that

participants can manage their own time. Placing the most important items at the start of the agenda insures that only the least important will be left unfinished.

18. Use a meeting evaluation checklist as an occasional spot check. Questions should be answered by each participant before leaving. Was the purpose of the meeting clear? Was the agenda received in advance? Were any materials essential for preparation also received in advance? Did the meeting start on time? If not, why not? Was the agenda followed adequately, or was the meeting allowed to wander from it unnecessarily? Was the purpose achieved? Were assignments and deadlines fixed where appropriate? Of the total meeting time, what percentage was not effectively utilized? Why? The evaluations, unsigned, should be collected for the chairman's immediate review.

After

19. Expedite the preparation of the minutes. Concise minutes should be completed and distributed within 24 hours if possible or 48 hours at the outside. If people can rely on receiving well-written minutes, those who really aren't needed will be freed from attending. Minutes are also a reminder and a useful followup tool, as shown in the next suggestion.

20. Insure that progress reports are made and decisions executed. Provide followup to insure the implementation of decisions and checks on progress where warranted. Uncompleted actions should be listed under "Unfinished Business" on the next meeting's agenda.

21. Make a committee inventory. Survey all committees, investigating whether their objectives have been achieved and if not when they can be expected to be. Abolish those that have accomplished their intended purpose.

Chapter 6

Handling

Decisions

"The biggest thief of time is indecision," says Charles Flory. Arriving at the point of decision, many managers vacillate, procrastinate, or in other ways refuse to decide. Not only does indecision waste time; it involves worry. It may cause worry, result from it, or simply accompany it. And worry is so destructive that it makes a man tired before he starts his day's work.

Furthermore, as Frank Nunlist points out, by making a decision faster you have more time to correct it if it *is* wrong. You also save the time that might be spent in subsequent meetings held for the purpose of reconsidering and debating the facts. If the decision has already been made, such meetings are unnecessary.

From an objective point of view, postponing a decision may be the worst alternative a manager could choose in terms of his company's welfare. So important is the timing of a decision in some situations that *any* resolution of a problem is better than none. It is easy to see that the best decision made too late is—well, too late. What is more difficult to accept is that a bad decision is often better than none. Auren Uris argues that if you are truly committed to a course of action and announce it with confidence, you can make it work.[1] We know that what is done is often less important than how. Many of the great leaders in history, though in doubt about a decision, would move ahead without further hesitation once they had made it. The resolving of doubts and the determination to pursue the course outlined have a mobilizing effect on all pertinent forces, and the chances of success become immeasurably enhanced.

There is a myth that delay improves the quality of decisions. Flory, from the experience of many years as a consultant to executives, says that 15 percent of the problems coming to an executive need to mature, 5 percent shouldn't be answered at all, and the remaining 80 percent should be decided *now*. But managers *don't* decide now.

Needing more facts is a convenient excuse for this action. Those who insist on having all the facts before making a decision should remember the Pareto principle: if 20 percent of the facts are critical to 80 percent of the outcome, and you have these critical facts, then waiting until all the facts are in can be absurd. This practice has been dubbed "paralysis of analysis."

Delays in decision making are also to be expected when decision-making power is split or the locus of the authority is unclear. It is quite understandable that managers who are unsure of their authority would be reluctant to make decisions. Refine your organization table and job descriptions to clarify decision-making responsibility. This will prevent executives from avoiding or delaying decisions because others are involved.

Fear of Mistakes

The real causes of indecision may lie much deeper than the reasons given for it. The manager wishes something would happen so he wouldn't have to decide. He lacks confidence in his ability no matter how many facts are available. He is afraid of making a mistake.

Yet few leaders and few organizations have avoided mistakes. Some of the best-managed corporations have fallen into "million-dollar mistakes" that have been joked about. The key is not that mistakes were made but that something worthwhile was learned, sometimes opening the door to larger successes. For many managers, being fired has been the best thing that ever happened to them. Thomas Huxley said:

> Next to being right, the best of all things is to be clearly and definitely wrong, because you will come out somewhere. If you go buzzing about between right and wrong, vibrating and fluctuating, you come out nowhere; but if you are absolutely and thoroughly wrong, you must have the good fortune of knocking against the fact that sets you all straight again.[2]

If you are afraid of the consequences of a mistake, you are timid. Perhaps experience has shown you that despite high-sounding phrases to the contrary, top management simply doesn't like mistakes, so the smart boys don't stick their necks out. Edward Bursk and Charles Ford found that

> Many executives operate under the theory that the fewer controversial decisions they make, the less they will have to accept responsibility for a wrong one. Often a decision hangs in limbo while executives try to get someone else to affix his imprimatur to it and thus to take the responsibility for it. . . . The fear of making a mistake encourages the quest for an inordinate amount of information and supporting data by the decision-maker. Hence, decisions that could be made speedily with a minimum amount of data are delayed pending the development of more and more information, most of which frequently reconfirms what the decision-maker already knows.[3]

Risk is implicit in all decisions. There are no riskless decisions. Nor will an executive ever have all the facts. He must decide without all the facts. As Peter Drucker says, too many managers look on a decision as a problem rather than an opportunity. As a result they tend to settle for the solution with

the lowest cost even though it promises the lowest gains.
Every decision is an attempt to balance gains, costs, and
risks.[4]

Fear of failure may so immobilize a manager that he is
prevented not only from making decisions himself but also
from delegating them, afraid that mistakes made by subordinates will reflect on him. Thus the error-avoidance philosophy seeps down through the ranks, generating a pervasive
caution that atrophies an entire organization. "The rude truth
is," says Charles Ford, "decisions are hard to get in business
today." [5] Executive timidity results from unwritten corporate
policies of risk avoidance that frown on mistakes in any form.
The ability to make those fast, everyday gut decisions that
keep a business moving is becoming a lost art through disuse.
"I'm waiting for so-and-so." "I need more information."
"We're still thinking about it." "These things take time."

What escapes the nondecider is that his procrastination
should be viewed as a decision by default. It's a decision *not*
to decide.

THE MEANING OF MISTAKES

Progressive companies encourage risk taking. It is axiom-
atic that we often learn more from our mistakes than from
our successes. David Emery suggests that a manager "should
not only *not* penalize employees for mistakes made in attempts to improve, but should reward them in some appropriate form. One of the greatest unmeasured losses in business," he says, "are the unrealized innovations inhibited by
fear lest the attempt prove a failure." [6]

As a practical matter, we do find a pattern in the handling
of mistakes. Stupid or repeated mistakes are punished. Honest mistakes are tolerated. Venture mistakes, if the results
are not disastrous, are applauded. "Call your men in," advises
Saul Gellerman, "and ask them to tell you about the last
'good' error they made." If they can't think of one, you have a
real problem. No one making no mistakes can be attempting
much that's really worthwhile.

Intelligent tolerance of mistakes, continues Gellerman, is at the center of the problem of motivating people. "If management is to motivate through challenge, it must insist on risk, which involves the distinct possibility of failure." [7] An organization that is making no mistakes is either taking no risks or dead. What counts is not the mistakes but what is learned from them.

Setting Deadlines

It is common for managers to fail to set deadlines on all decisions and stick to them. The imposition of due dates is mandatory for time management. When delegating a task or scheduling the steps to be taken toward an objective—set deadlines.

No delegation is complete until the assignment has been defined, the person responsible notified, and the deadline set. A project will almost always be completed sooner if it has a deadline date than if it hasn't.

The way a deadline is set may make a considerable difference in the attitude of the person responsible for meeting it. If it is difficult to attain or unreasonable or if it is imposed without discussion, resentment is almost sure to follow. Just as goals and objectives that are jointly determined will generate commitment on the part of those who are to achieve them, so with a deadline: a date set cooperatively will be more enthusiastically pursued.

Deadlines work well because scheduling is generally a people problem. But suppose the deadlines are imposed without regard for human tolerance. With adequate stimulus anyone can rise to an emergency and perform at a peak energy level for a short time. But if you try to program the emergency-level output on a regular basis, people will know it and resist.

Deadlines work best, then, when they are self-imposed and are viewed as reasonable and equitable. When these ingredients go into their setting, their utility as time savers has been proved many times.

UNREALISTIC TIME ESTIMATES

One of the problems with setting deadlines is unrealistic
time estimates. Poor projections lead to frustration and often
to panic and crisis. I was guilty of such an unrealistic estimate a few years ago when leaving my office for a talk in
New Orleans. I had unwisely postponed till the last minute
several items that really needed to be done before my depar-
ture. Leaving a few minutes later than I would normally, I
jumped into a cab and asked the driver if he could make La-
Guardia Airport by 3:00. The motor was not running, and the
driver made no move to start it. Instead he put both hands on
the wheel and slowly turned around to look at me. "Mister,"
he said, "you see Fifth Avenue?"

"Yes, yes," I responded, "I see Fifth Avenue. How about
the airport?"

"You see the traffic, mister? This is the week before Christ-
mas. We're lucky if we get across Fifth Avenue in 15 minutes.
At times like this you've just got to allow more time."

The cab driver had given me a basic lesson in time management. He couldn't know the reason for my chuckle as we
drove off, so I explained. The subject of my talk to the group
of chief executives in New Orleans: "Managing Your Time,
the Chief Executive's Most Critical Resource."

Most managers, when asked to list what they expect to do
tomorrow, start writing down not one day's work but three or
four days'. They generally underestimate time requirements
by an appalling margin and make no allowance for interruptions and emergencies totally unrelated to the tasks they set
out to accomplish.

On the way to work, many a manager will think optimisti-
cally of the great day he's going to have. With the warm glow
of breakfast still hovering over him, his thoughts take wings.
By the time he has arrived at the office, a month's work has
been pictured, including the first steps on a number of projects long postponed.

Then comes reality. A breakdown on the night shift means
that two emergency orders are delayed and the gloomy mar-

keting vice-president is standing at the machine as the manager walks in. Two hours later, when he finally gets to his office, five phone calls and three people are waiting for him. Another one of those days.

On the way home for a late dinner, he strums the steering wheel with his fingers and ponders, "Let's see, now. What were those things I told myself I was going to get done today?"

The secret of deadlines is not entirely in setting the time. It's also in building in a "contingency factor." Allowing no time for your own errors, errors of others, or common misfortune is unrealistic. The Canadian managers proposing that 20 percent of their day *not* be planned were anticipating the emergency—expecting the unexpected.

RESPONSE DEADLINES

When a time limit is set on a decision, the person making the decision should have the authority to place time limits on any help or information he needs in order to achieve his objective. This should apply up and down the chain of command; he should be able to require the necessary action from appropriate parties above as well as below himself in the organization.

Charles Ford has related this question to the tempo of decision making in a company. "There is probably a greater relationship between business success and fast tempo," says Ford, "than with any other single factor." [8] He defines "tempo" as the speed with which an organization identifies problems and opportunities and makes and implements decisions. To determine the tempo of your organization, says Ford, take a number of recent, important decisions your company has made and determine when the events that necessitated them first occurred.

1. Suppose that the very life of your company depended on its reaching those decisions in one-half or one-third the time. Could they have been made?

2. Take three recent decisions resulting in projects undertaken—involving, for example, a new product, a new marketing approach, or new equipment. How much time elapsed between decision and implementation or completion? Again, if the company's life depended on its cutting the time by one-half or one-third, could it have done so? Consider what benefits would have accrued if the time had indeed been cut.

3. Take the last time your company was rocked by competition. How much time did it take to find out about the impending threat? Could this time have been shortened? Could your company have reacted faster with quicker, more alert feedback?

4. Do all employees of your company act as though they were in a hurry to get things done? Are they bothered by things pending and unfinished?

If your answer to the time-cutting parts of the first three questions is yes and to the last question is no, chances are you have a tempo problem, and its causes are well worth analyzing. Knowing that one has a problem is one thing; knowing why is quite another.

A packaging firm in the Northeast was described by Ford as having a very serious tempo problem. Although the company had all the ingredients for success, things just didn't seem to be getting done fast enough. The president established a system of time limits. Every memo, every project, every request for a quotation, and so forth carried a time limit imposed by the originator. With strict enforcement the drift stopped. Answers were fed back quickly. Things got done more rapidly.

The right to set deadlines was extended to lower echelons. If the shipping manager proposed a new type of container and wanted executive appproval, he time-limited his request. So did a salesman who wanted an answer to some questions from a superior. Even the president was subjected to time limits by subordinates.

The key to this program was enforcement. When the pattern had been established, it sustained itself on the visible signs of accomplishment. The result was a markedly quickened tempo and an accelerated company growth.[9]

The hapless manager who must wait for information or decisions before acting also has another powerful tool at his disposal: the "unless I hear" memo. Having outlined a proposal for action, he simply states something like the following: "Unless I hear to the contrary, I will proceed on this basis on Wednesday of next week."

Chapter 7

Delegating

We have heard about delegation. We have read about delegation. We have thought about delegation. How many of us know an executive who has studied delegation and set about to practice what he learned? Not many, I fear. Even those who teach management professionally encounter few serious conversations on the subject. The concept of delegation as a vital tool for the effective manager seems rarely to be grasped.

This omission is a serious error. Managing is generally defined as getting things done through people. Delegation essentially is giving people things to do. Thus by definition the two are inextricably interwoven. We must conclude that a manager who does not delegate is not managing. Of course, since there are degrees of effectiveness, a more precise statement would be that one who cannot delegate effectively cannot manage effectively. Delegation then must be, of all of the skills and activities of the manager, one of the most indispensable. It is surprising, say William Newman, Charles Summer, and E. Kirby Warren, that such a fundamental aspect of organization continues to be misunderstood and to be inefficiently handled.[1]

As a key activity of the manager, delegation has benefits both direct and derived. Four of the most significant are that delegation

1. Extends results from what a man can do to what he can control,

2. Releases time for more important work,

3. Develops subordinates' initiative, skill, knowledge, and competence, and

4. Maintains decision level.

The Myth of Decision Level

Few managers ever think consciously about decision level. This neglect is strange because practically all agree with the fundamental principle that decisions ought to be delegated to the lowest possible level where they can be made intelligently and where the relevant facts and required judgment to make sound decisions are available. But managers fail to equate the maintenance of appropriate decision level with effective delegation.

It is not true that the higher the level at which a decision is made, the better the quality of the decision. The real key here is the type of decision. For example, policy clearly must be set at top levels because of the span of experience, perspective, and information available. However, operating decisions, involving problems at lower levels in the organization, are often far better if they are made where the facts and the special expertise are available.

Decision level seems to be considered an idle theory that sounds right but has little practical application. What a mistake! Listen to Saxon Tate, managing director of Canada and Dominion Sugar: "Decisions simply must be made at the lowest possible level for management at the top to maintain its effectiveness. I make few decisions with a time span of less than a year. At one point I made them for as short a time span as one week. I now see that kind of involvement in detail as a luxury no man at the top can afford."

Managing Versus Operating

Examples of managers who could not relinquish operating responsibilities are abundant. Companies have often promoted their best salesman into their worst sales manager. The tragedy is of course double. They have lost their best salesman, and worse, they now have the wrong man in a higher and more important post.

Laurence Peter and Raymond Hull developed the "Peter principle" from observing the regularity with which good teachers were promoted to school principalships without any regard for their supervisory qualifications.[2] Church conferences have long been plagued by a habit of electing their most popular local pastors to critical administrative positions. These churchmen usually come without any experience in administration other than in their local church. The unfairness to the entire denomination is exceeded only by the unfairness to the individual himself.

I once talked with such a clergyman. In his new post he was responsible for a number of corporate entities and a multimillion-dollar consolidated budget, and yet he had no authority to make significant decisions. Problems of enormous complexity, both managerial and operational, assailed him daily. Virtually none of his previous experience was helpful. Had he only known, he confessed to me, what the future held in store, he would never have accepted the "honor."

Peter and Hull cite an interesting example of a mechanic with outstanding ability to diagnose obscure faults and endless patience in correcting them. He was made a foreman, but his love of things mechanical and his perfectionism were liabilities in his new position. He undertook personally any job that looked interesting no matter how busy he was. "I'll work it in somehow," he said. Never letting a piece of work go until he was fully satisfied with it, he meddled, tinkered, and checked constantly. He was seldom at his desk because he was usually up to his elbows in dismantled motors, while men who should have been doing the work stood by watching, and others sat around waiting to be assigned new tasks. As a result the shop was always overcrowded with work and in a muddle, and delivery dates were always missed.

Our mechanic-turned-foreman could not understand that the average customer cared less about complete perfection than about getting his car back on time. Nor could he understand that most of his men were less interested in motors than in paychecks. So he didn't get along with his customers, his subordinates, or his boss. He was a competent mechanic. He became an incompetent foreman.

What does this say for our up-from-the-ranks system? It seems clear that good doers are not necessarily good managers—and good managers not necessarily good doers. How much are we losing every day by promoting men beyond their areas of competence, relying on past records and giving no thought to the requirements of the new job?

The basic trouble, contend Peter and Hull, is that most promotion practices are simply rewards for good performance. Pay differentials ought to be geared to the quality of a man's work rather than to seniority or rank. An exceptional employee should be able to earn more than a supervisor without being promoted to a position for which he is unqualified.[3]

Visualize the organization chart tipped on its side, with the chief executive and his officers at one end and the ranks of workers at the other. Movement on the chart then becomes lateral rather than upward and represents the concept of matching talent and experience with job requirements.

Jewel Companies is said to have gone even farther. The president turned his organization chart upside down. At the bottom of the V he placed the chief executive—himself. This reversal indicated that the manager's job was to assist those "above" him in being more effective. Supervisors supported the workers, who were doing the most important job—producing the goods to fill customer needs. The workers occupied positions at the *top* of the chart.

ARE YOU MANAGING OR DOING?

Raymond Loen provided the Business Management Council with a very interesting analysis of managing versus doing.[4] Getting bogged down in *doing* jobs instead of *managing* them, he feels, is one of the chief causes of lack of productivity on the part of managers. Their own experience often holds them back. Since they have pulled themselves up to where they are by excelling in a particular specialty, they continue doing the things they have always done well. They hang on to old attitudes that have made them successful as doers but that are stones around their necks as managers—for example, a self-image as experts who can outperform their people.

They are aware that they are supposed to be leaders. The semantics of the word "leader" suggests that followers have confidence in *him*. This notion torpedoes·what a manager is supposed to do: help his people have confidence in *themselves*. His responsibility is to get results through others.

This is not to say a manager should always manage and never do. He should know, however, whether his doing activities are important ones. For example, a company president who came up through the sales side of the business subconsciously felt that marketing was where the company's main problems were, and he spent 57 percent of his time doing clerical or routine work in various marketing areas. In another case a top financial officer of a major firm felt that the best way to control costs was to approve personally the hundreds of requisitions that came to his department—including nominal raises for clerical people. For both of these executives, the chosen work was easy, it was familiar to them, and undoubtedly it made them feel more productive. At least it made them feel more comfortable than trying to do the real work of a manager, for which they apparently had little skill.

Unfortunately, it is not easy to separate managing from doing in typical daily activities. There is much confusion between performing a basic operational function (marketing, production, or engineering) and managing the function (planning, organizing, and controlling it). To test your impression of what is managing and what is doing, examine the 12 tasks in the following list, drawn up by Loen:

1. Calling on an account with one of your people in order to show the account that your company's top management is interested in him.
2. Deciding whether to add a position.
3. Approving a request from one of your people for a routine expenditure.
4. Reviewing monthly reports to determine progress toward achieving specific objectives for your area of responsibility.
5. Deciding what the cost budget shall be for your area of responsibility.
6. Interviewing a prospective employee referred to you by a friend.
7. Attending an industry conference to learn the latest in technical developments.
8. Meeting with an outside specialist to design a profit-sharing plan.
9. Explaining to one of your people why he is receiving a raise.
10. Asking one of your people what he thinks about an idea you have for his area of responsibility.
11. Entertaining the officer of a large supplier with whom you are negotiating.
12. Giving a talk to the local chamber of commerce about your company's plans and purposes.[5]

Now check your responses against Loen's answers and explanations:

1. *Doing.* It may be highly necessary to make such a call but it is clearly selling or public relations, not managing. The direct purpose of the call is not to get results through others.
2. *Managing.* This is developing the organization structure.
3. *Doing.* Since the expenditure is a routine one, the executive should probably delegate this function and arrange for a periodic audit to be sure that correct procedures are followed.
4. *Managing.* This is measuring and evaluating.
5. *Managing.* This is planning—developing a budget.
6. *Doing.* This is performing a personnel function—even

though it's undoubtedly the considerate thing to do. Deciding to hire someone *after* all the recruiting and selecting had been done, however, would be staffing, a managing activity.

7. *Doing.* Since the stated intent is to learn the latest *technical* developments, it is questionable whether this will help the executive increase the results he gets through others.

8. *Doing.* Designing a profit-sharing plan is a personnel or finance function.

9. *Managing.* This is motivating.

10. *Managing.* This is communicating, probably in order to develop a program. It could be a form of motivating if the purpose is to get participation now in order to get acceptance later.

11. *Doing.* This is an activity within the field of purchasing or buying.

12. *Doing.* This is a public relations function.[6]

What then is *managing?* Planning, organizing, staffing, directing, and controlling the activities of others in order to achieve objectives that have been agreed on.[7] Specifically this involves:

Planning. Forecasting, setting objectives, developing strategies, programming, budgeting, setting procedures, determining policies.

Organizing. Establishing the organization structure, delineating relationships, creating position descriptions, establishing position qualifications.

Staffing. Selecting, orienting, training, developing.

Directing. Delegating, motivating, coordinating, managing differences, managing change.

Controlling. Establishing a reporting system, developing performance standards, measuring results, taking corrective action, rewarding performance.

Making decisions. Collecting facts, specifying problems, setting goals, generating alternatives, evaluating consequences, selecting a course, and implementing.

Communicating. Transmitting messages, testing reception, clarifying messages, checking feedback.

What then is *operating?* The direct business functions have been described as the operational functions of management. Each of these is divided below into its constituent activities:

Research and development. Basic R&D, applied R&D, production engineering—design, test, followup.

Production. Plant engineering, industrial engineering, purchasing, production planning and control, manufacturing, quality control.

Marketing. Market research, advertising, sales planning, sales promotion, sales operations, physical distribution.

Finance. Financial planning and relations, tax management, custody of funds, credit and collections, insurance.

Control. General accounting, cost accounting, budget planning and control, internal auditing, systems and procedures.

Personnel administration. Employment, wage and salary administration, industrial relations, organization planning and development, employee services.

External relations. Public relations, creditor and investor communications, civic affairs, association and community relations.

Legal and corporate relations. Corporate legal matters, patents, employee legal questions, stockholder relations, board of directors activities, corporation secretarial affairs.

The Effect of Management Level on Time Allocation

To know how much he should delegate is a difficult problem for the manager. Management level affects this problem in at least two ways. The first is that the ideal ratio between managing and operating time varies directly with the management level. The second is that the allocations of time to the specific managerial functions such as planning are not in fixed percentages but vary with industry or type of organization, type of personnel, characteristics of both leaders and followers, and nature of the situations or tasks involved.

The higher one goes on the management ladder, the less time he should spend operating and the more managing. Exhibit 10, adapted from an early version by Ralph Davis and since improved by Louis Allen, shows the changing proportions of the manager's work recommended for operating and managing at various levels in the organization.

Since planning time increases with the management level, it seems reasonable to assume that controlling time would also, though possibly to a lesser degree. If both of these functions expand significantly, something has to diminish. In the

Exhibit 10. Proportions of managing and operating work at various management levels.

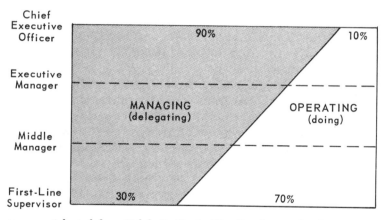

SOURCE: Adapted from Ralph C. Davis, *The Fundamentals of Top Management* (New York: Harper & Bros., 1951).

absence of definitive research on the matter, it may be supposed that time spent organizing and staffing might remain fairly constant while that spent in the various activities of directing would decrease. One can also conclude (in line with Saxon Tate's observations on page 123) that the higher the level of management decisions, the fewer in number, the greater in time span, and the more planning-oriented they will be.

No doubt the particular leadership style of the manager would influence the changing ratio shown in Exhibit 10. For instance, the entrepreneurial boss with "a finger in every pie" would tend to continue to operate rather than manage and might well neglect planning and control functions. On the other hand, radical variations in the situation could be a very strong determinant in how much time an executive devotes to each of those functions. For example, the financial plight of the small college today clearly calls for the president to re-double his development and fund-raising efforts.

To facilitate the visualization of the impact of management levels on the relative allocation of the executive's time to managerial and operational functions, a time management cone is shown in Exhibit 11. The cone makes it clear that dif-ferent managers, depending on their assignments within the organization, will engage in completely different operating activities but similar managerial activities. A single job, par-ticularly at a lower supervisory level, would not encompass all the operational functions or activities. As the supervisor moves up the ladder, however, his job would tend to em-brace more and more of the activities shown.

This representation of the time cone furnishes perspective on the changing nature of jobs as one rises in management. Changes occur in the duties of the job itself (the plant fore-man's job is quite different from the lathe operator's and the production manager's from the night foreman's). Changes also occur in the proportions of time allocated to managing by contrast with operating and to the distinct managerial func-tions.

For example, observe on the cone the steadily increasing time required for planning. Consider the operational function of external relations. Time for this activity may not appear on the managerial scene until the top executive level is reached, and it may not be significant—except in the case of a vice-president for public relations—in any post below the chief executive's. But at this level, and particularly in marketing-oriented enterprises, this duty may assume a commanding proportion of the radically reduced operational time segment. What better way of reminding top executives who are busy "riding their specialties" that they are not spending their time where the payoff will be greatest?

Exhibit 11. The managerial time cone.

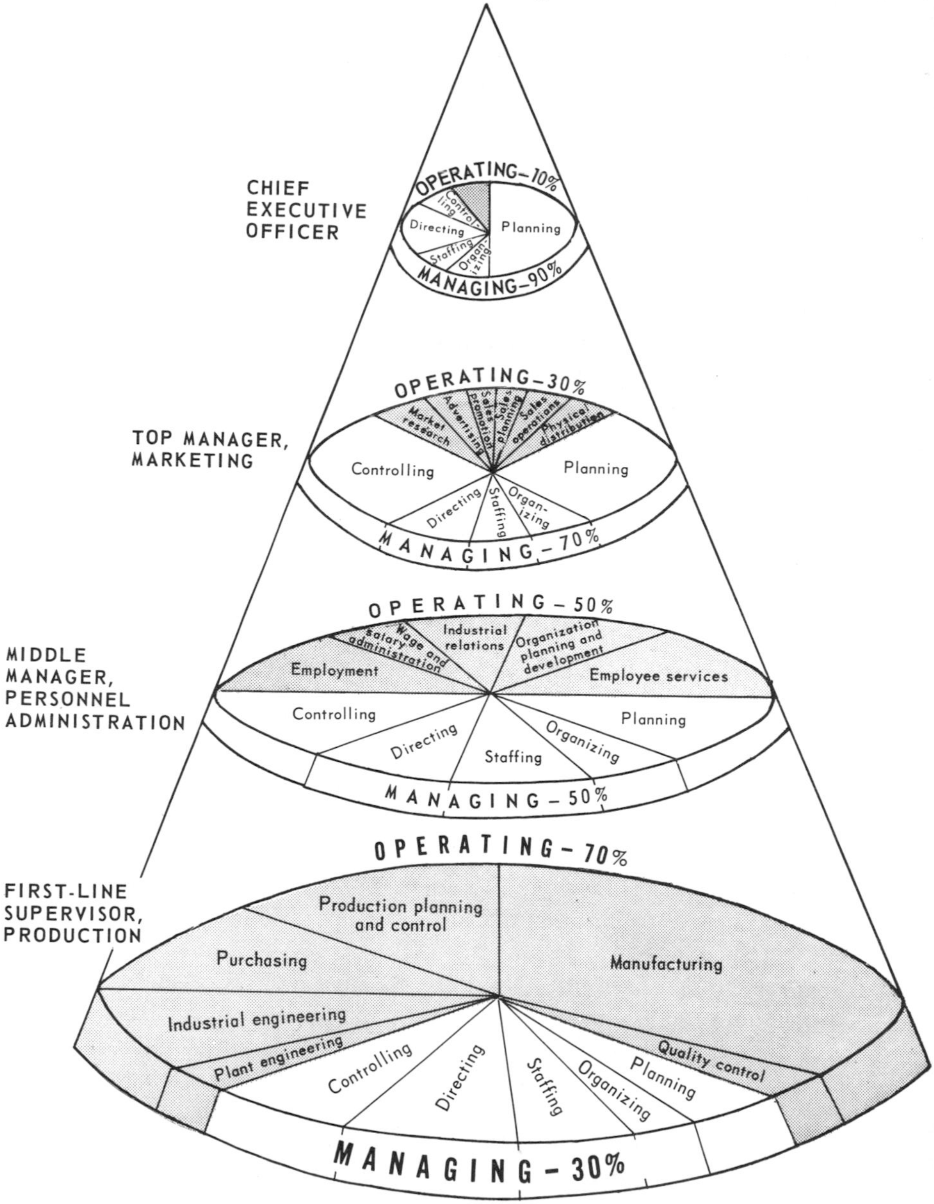

CHIEF EXECUTIVE OFFICER
OPERATING–10%
Controlling / Directing / Staffing / Organizing / Planning
MANAGING–90%

TOP MANAGER, MARKETING
OPERATING–30%
Market research / Advertising / Sales promotion / Sales operations / Physical distribution
Controlling / Directing / Staffing / Organizing / Planning
MANAGING–70%

MIDDLE MANAGER, PERSONNEL ADMINISTRATION
OPERATING–50%
Wage and salary administration / Industrial relations / Organization planning and development / Employment / Employee services
Controlling / Directing / Staffing / Organizing / Planning
MANAGING–50%

FIRST-LINE SUPERVISOR, PRODUCTION
OPERATING–70%
Production planning and control / Purchasing / Manufacturing / Industrial engineering / Plant engineering / Quality control / Controlling / Directing / Staffing / Organizing / Planning
MANAGING–30%

SOURCE: Adapted from "The Time Management Cone," in R. Alec Mackenzie, *Managing Time at the Top* (New York: The Presidents Association, 1970). Copyright © 1972 by R. Alec Mackenzie.

Barriers to Delegation

The essential tool for the executive to use in managing his time is delegation. Yet this tool is rarely exploited well, as we saw at the beginning of the chapter. Its necessity is rarely understood. There are critical barriers to effective delegation in the delegator, the delegatee, and the situation. The lists below itemize several problems already examined along with a number of others, some meriting special comment. They will be discussed in the following sections.

BARRIERS IN THE DELEGATOR

1. Preference for operating
2. Demand that everyone "know all the details"
3. "I can do it better myself" fallacy
4. Lack of experience in the job or in delegating
5. Insecurity
6. Fear of being disliked
7. Refusal to allow mistakes
8. Lack of confidence in subordinates
9. Perfectionism, leading to overcontrol
10. Lack of organizational skill in balancing workloads
11. Failure to delegate authority commensurate with responsibility
12. Uncertainty over tasks and inability to explain
13. Disinclination to develop subordinates
14. Failure to establish effective controls and to follow up

BARRIERS IN THE DELEGATEE

1. Lack of experience
2. Lack of competence
3. Avoidance of responsibility
4. Overdependence on the boss
5. Disorganization
6. Overload of work
7. Immersion in trivia

BARRIERS IN THE SITUATION

1. One-man-show policy
2. No toleration of mistakes
3. Criticality of decisions
4. Urgency, leaving no time to explain (crisis management)
5. Confusion in responsibilities and authority
6. Understaffing

OPERATING PRIORITY

Louis Allen's "principle of operating priority" states that "When called upon to perform both management work and operating work during the same period, a manager will tend to give first priority to operating work."[8] Charles Flory has observed this syndrome particularly among profession-oriented managers—the engineer who can't leave his slide rule inside his desk or the chemist who can't stay out of the lab.

The operating priority may be imposed on managers by their superiors. When a boss insists that his team members know all the details of what is going on, he forces them into operating work by making it impossible for them to delegate. They can know the details only if they are actively involved in them.

A humorous portrayal of operating priority has been captured by the author of the anonymous "Functions of an Executive":

As nearly everyone knows, an executive has practically nothing to do, except
　　to decide what is to be done;
　　to tell somebody to do it;
　　to listen to reasons why it should not be done, why it should be done by someone else, or why it should be done in a different way;
　　to follow up to see if the thing has been done;
　　to discover it has not been done;
　　to inquire why it has not been done;
　　to listen to excuses from the person who should have done it;
　　to follow up again to see if the thing has been done, only to discover it has been done incorrectly;

to point out how it should have been done;

to conclude that as long as it has been done it might as well be left where it is;

to wonder if it is time to get rid of a person who cannot do a thing right;

to reflect that he probably has a wife and large family, and certainly any successor would be just as bad and maybe worse;

to consider how much simpler and better the thing would have been done if one had done it oneself in the first place;

to reflect sadly that one could have done it right in 20 minutes, and now one has to spend two days to find out why it has taken three weeks for somebody else to do it wrong.

THE FALLACY OF OMNIPOTENCE

The fallacy of omnipotence—otherwise known as the "I can do it better myself" fallacy—is often found among young entrepreneurs. Their ability, determination, and vitality have provided the essential ingredients for the crucial beginning and growth periods of a new business. The same characteristics, however, make effective delegation extremely difficult, and they operate as detrimental forces in the maturing organization.

It is understandable that the qualities directly responsible for the success of the company should be constantly defended by the entrepreneur. It is equally understandable that these very qualities can lead to the feeling that no one else could do a task quite so effectively. The problem with this reasoning is that every time the manager fails to explain a task to a subordinate and if necessary to coach him through it, he insures that the next time he will have to be the one to do it again. No one else has learned how.

Even if the entrepreneur can do a better job, the choice is not between the quality of his work and the quality of the subordinate's; it is rather between the benefits of his better performance on a single task and the benefits derived from his devoting that time to planning, delegating, supervising, and coaching, to training and developing a team. Eventually such a team will both outperform and outlast the entrepreneur.

We are reminded of one of the principal values of delegation —the extension of results from what a person can do to what he can control. Successful delegation doubles, triples, and raises even more the output of one man as soon as he begins to achieve his results through the multiplied efforts of others.

FEAR OF BEING DISLIKED

While seldom talked about and almost never admitted, the fear of being disliked or resented by subordinates is a factor of substantial proportions in many managers. The senior who has this problem carries a bulging briefcase home so he won't ruin an assistant's weekend. It would be interesting to know how many of the subordinates treated so tenderly actually like their boss or at least do not lose their respect for him.

In a reported study by John Hemphill at Ohio State University, 500 groups of supervisors and managers were rated by their subordinates. The leaders who were rated good or excellent were the ones who made the greatest use of delegation. Conversely, leaders who were scored poor were ineffective as delegators.[9]

LACK OF CONFIDENCE IN SUBORDINATES

Lack of confidence in subordinates is of course one of the primary barriers to delegation. Few managers, however, recognize that the cause of this condition lies in themselves. If subordinates do not have skills and competence warranting appropriate delegation, the manager has failed to carry out his responsibilities either by not staffing with competent people or by not training and developing his team.

William Newman has recorded some of the comments that betray a lack of confidence: "He'll take care of the details all right, but he'll miss the main point." "I'm not sure of his judgment in a pinch." "He has ideas but doesn't follow through." "He's too young to command the respect of other men."[10]

The remedy for this attitude may sound easy—either train your subordinates to be more effective or replace them with abler people. But often the situation is not so clear-cut. To be confident of subordinates requires accurate knowledge of their capabilities and characteristics. Assessing potential and evaluating management performance are not easy tasks. Most managers know too little about their subordinates' real capacities. Therefore, lack of confidence in many cases is not justified. Delegating to the ablest or most capable man on your team can have an overall detrimental effect: the strong get stronger and the weak get weaker, and those who need the experience don't get it. Also, you are in danger of distributing the workload unfairly, in effect penalizing your best people.

When delegation is withheld because of lack of confidence, subordinates are denied the opportunity to develop the very ability they need to warrant the confidence. This makes the manager's doubts about them a self-fulfilling prophecy. The only way to know what men can really do is to try them. You are likely to find that most if not all of them have hidden potential. They can do things you never suspected. They need only to be given a chance.

Reverse Delegation

An interesting phenomenon in manager-subordinate relations is what is often called reverse delegation, or delegation up. The subtlety of this practice is well described by David Jaquith. When he assumed the presidency of Vega Industries a number of years ago, he succeeded a chief executive who had been a veritable one-man show. The former president had made all the decisions. A steady stream of managers had come into his office with questions and left with answers.

When confronted with the first few such questions, Jaquith didn't have the answers on the tip of his tongue. So for a time he responded with "Well, leave it here. I'll have something for you on Monday." One Saturday afternoon while he was working at his desk, he realized that he was alone in the office. The following Monday he asked where everyone was and was told with some surprise that of course Saturday was everybody's "golfing day." The more Jaquith thought about the situation, the less he liked it. He considered the principle that managers are supposed to get things done through others. The question then arose in his mind: who is getting things done through whom in this office?

A little mulling and he came up with a sign for his desk that read: "DBMP—BMA." When the next question was brought to him, he pointed to the sign and explained its meaning: "Don't bring me problems—bring me answers."

"Yes, you do have a problem, don't you?" became his standard response to subordinates wanting his decision. "What are you going to do about it?" would follow. Instead of an answerer, Jaquith became a questioner.

Auren Uris points out that there are times when it is appropriate to delegate up, as when a situation calls for:

1. Praise or reward; honor won by a subordinate can have greater weight if announced by the executive's boss.

2. Approval or backing; when hiring a man with whom both the executive and his boss will be working, it may be appropriate to have the boss cooperate in the selection process.

3. Critical decisions and special abilities; where decisions are being made in critical areas where the boss has unusually important expertise, his participation in the decision may be most appropriate.

4. Full weight of authority; in certain instances the announcement of a new policy may be given greater weight or its importance may be more enhanced by having it come from the boss.[11]

In all such cases the upward delegation of authority ought to be considered carefully and used sparingly.

WHY REVERSE DELEGATION TAKES PLACE

At least six reasons that reverse delegation occurs can be identified:

1. *The subordinate wishes to avoid risk.* It is easier to ask the boss than to decide for himself. Asking the boss is a way of sharing if not shedding the responsibility, and over a period of time, it becomes a habit of dependence. To break the

habit, simply refuse to decide for a subordinate. Ask simple questions such as "What is your recommendation?"

2. *The subordinate is afraid of criticism,* especially negative, unreasonable, or public criticism. Constructive criticism should be offered in private.

3. *The subordinate lacks confidence,* which can only come from experience and knowledge. To develop it requires more than telling a subordinate he's good. He must be given experience with increasingly difficult problems to help him sense his own potentialities and see the effectiveness of his actions.

4. *The subordinate lacks the necessary information and resources* to accomplish the job successfully. No responsibility should be delegated without the requisite tools and authority.

5. *The boss wants to "be needed."* This attitude is impossible to hide from the subordinate. The boss may feel that making subordinates' decisions himself demonstrates his indispensability. These will be brought to him readily by staff members who are eager to share the risk.

6. *The boss is unable to say no to requests for help.* The trend toward participative management has encouraged bosses to think in terms of support and assistance to their subordinates. The boss who is unable to say no invites reverse delegation.

A boss's mere expression of an opinion can be interpreted as a decision—even a direct order—by a staff member caught in the clutches of risk avoidance. A simple, innocent-sounding query from a subordinate, "Could you give me an opinion on this?" has led many a manager into decision making below his level. Not that this was the manager's intent or even necessarily the subordinate's. Human nature being what it is, why should anyone, given an opinion by his boss, do other than assume that it has all the characteristics of a decision? How can he go wrong? If the decision turns out well, the subordinate can take credit for it. If it turns out badly, he can say with apparent justification that it was recommended by the boss.

Reverse delegation is occurring to managers daily at every level and in every type of business. And the chances are that few if any of those to whom it is happening have ever given it a thought. Alvin Eurich, president of the Academy for Educational Development, has a sign on his desk that reads, "What is your recommendation?" Such a sign might be a start. When the subordinate comes up with a recommendation but then wants *it* approved, the manager might say, "I see nothing wrong with your decision, but it's your responsibility. You will be living with the results. If you think that's the way to go, we'll move ahead."

Accountability for Delegated Responsibilities

There is a myth that by delegating the manager can avoid responsibility and consequent worry. Assigning duties to others is not a passport to freedom from worry and responsibility. This escape hatch is abdication, not delegation. Ultimate accountability rests permanently and ineluctably with the man at the top.

David Brown cautions that the delegator must think through how he will act if he discovers that things have not gone as they should. He must realize that the actions taken by others may not be the same as those he himself would have taken. Perhaps, says Brown, the most difficult part of learning to delegate is learning to accomodate differences. It is easy to accept the idea that people are not the same; it is much harder to accept its application. There can be immense variations not only in the quality and quantity of work performed but also in the ways it is done. The manager must be prepared to accept and live with his subordinates' methods and decisions. It may be a very big order, but he cannot reap the benefits of delegation unless he is willing to accept the risks.[12]

Gerald Achenbach highlights the extent of the risks involved: "All the people who work for an executive are purely extensions of himself. The most appalling thought about it is that when you delegate you are putting your reputation and your career in the hands of other people. And they can ruin you if they are not the right people to start with, if you have not trained them properly, or if you fail to delegate properly."

Courage is required to take the risk of delegating. William Newman comments that executives typically have a "temperamental aversion to taking chances." Delegation is a calculated risk, he points out, and we must expect that over time the gains will offset the losses. We must see the risk and adjust emotionally as well as intellectually in order to delegate effectively.[13]

Rate Yourself as a Delegator

When David Barran was elevated in the Royal Dutch/Shell Group's worldwide operations to the position of chairman of the Committee of Managing Directors, an unusual tribute was paid him. In *The New York Times* column "Man in Business," he was described as a man of immense physical vitality whose tremendous drive could bring a heavy-going executive meeting to life and produce action. In seeking to pin down the main reasons for Barran's success, his aides constantly called attention to his ability to "delegate and forget." [14]

How does one know how well he is delegating? Many quizzes have been devised to give managers a reading on how they rate as a delegator. The following questionnaire, adapted from a list drawn up by an associate of mine, is fairly typical:

1. Do you take work home regularly?
2. Do you work longer hours than your subordinates?
3. Do you spend time doing for others what they could be doing for themselves?
4. When you return from an absence from the office, do you find the in basket too full?
5. Are you still handling activities and problems you had before your last promotion?
6. Are you often interrupted with queries or requests on going projects or assignments?
7. Do you spend time on routine details that others could handle?

8. Do you like to keep a finger in every pie?
9. Do you rush to meet deadlines?
10. Are you unable to keep on top of priorities?

If you answer yes to none or one of the questions, your rating is excellent in delegating. If your yes answers total two to four, you should improve your delegating. If they total five or more, you appear to have a serious problem delegating and should place highest priority on its solution.

A top insurance executive who had attended an advanced management seminar realized that he had just such a problem. Following one of the suggestions in the presentation on time management, he returned to his office determined to start delegating in earnest and, not incidentally, to do something about the tremendous amount of material flowing into his in box. He and his secretary listed every item that had come to his desk during the week he had been gone: phone calls, messages, memoranda, requests for information—everything. Beside each item on the list, he noted its relative importance, whether it could have been delegated, and if so to whom. He then sent all the assignable tasks to the people who could deal with them, attaching a note saying, "Please handle."

This executive described the reaction to the notes as follows: "Some dust was stirred up and we had a few discussions, but almost all the requested tasks were handled. Many of them were taken care of more effectively than if I had done them. It changed my whole outlook on my job and has made me far more effective."

Chapter 8

Managing the Time
of Subordinates

The principal of a high school was attending his second seminar on time management. He had come back, he said, for some things he had completely missed in the first one. How, he asked, do you prevent the solutions to your own time wasters from adding to the problems of your team? How can you delegate everything you shouldn't be doing to a staff already overloaded? And in the chain of delegation, what happens to the last guy who has no one to whom he can delegate?

To solve your own time problems at the expense of your team is of course sheer folly. It's self-defeating because it is your team members through whom you as manager accomplish your objectives. If their time problems are ignored, or even worsened, your own effectiveness will be severely limited.

Subordinates often need their manager's guidance to develop a time sensitivity. This means training their peripheral vision so that they will be alert to surrounding activities and their probable effect. It also means developing their sense of timing and their ability to estimate time requirements realistically. It means instilling an attitude of anticipation rather than reaction so that problems can be prevented instead of merely remedied. It means nurturing their consciousness of the importance of time to others—their awareness that the good of the team must prevail over the good of the individual.

Because there is a commonality of time use and abuse at all levels of management, the process of helping subordinates become time-sensitive might profitably begin with the time wasters the executive has identified in his own work life and, let's hope, overcome. How does a manager spot time wasters among the men on his team? Without repeating what has been said about your own time management, it should be pointed out that the time wasters that plague you may equally plague your subordinates. But the first of their problems may be—their boss.

Are You *Your Subordinates' Problem?*

The reason we deal first with *you* as a problem in your subordinates' time management is that bottlenecks occur at the top of bottles. A manager's own insensitivity to time creates problems for his team whether he wills it or not.

Honest lists of time wasters drafted by middle and lower managers usually include "the boss" among their chief time wasters. There is a basic reason for this: the numerous contacts of a subordinate with his boss provide many occasions for time waste. The complaints of subordinates in this regard are various. There are superiors who "want to visit about unimportant matters" or who have such a preoccupation with detail that they spend most of their time checking up on the work of subordinates. There is "the boss you can never see when you need him" and the one who is "constantly destroying your priorities with a list of new requests, often bearing little resemblance to priorities already assigned."

It is extremely important for the manager to be aware of the effect he has on his subordinates' time. There are three sins that are committed with wearying frequency—transmitting instructions poorly, keeping subordinates waiting, and interrupting their work.

COMMUNICATING INSTRUCTIONS POORLY

The quality of communications exerts a pervading influence in the management of subordinates' time. Meaningful relationships are impossible without effective communicating. Ross Barrett has identified two fundamental causes of waste of executive time in the course of ordinary communications: a disregard of subordinates' time needs by upper management and a lack of understanding and consideration on subordinates' part concerning a superior's time.[1]

Poor communications are evident in hasty, ill-conceived, and poorly worded instructions. Curiously, the hasty order is usually an order given in a hurry to save time. Ultimately it results in a confusion that takes longer to correct than it would have taken to insure understanding in the first place.

The investment of adequate time to give clear instructions leads to more effective communication and improved performance. There is no substitute for the delegator's making sure that the person who is to do the task understands (1) precisely what is expected, (2) the extent of his responsibility and exactly what authority is being delegated, and (3) when the assignment is to be completed.

KEEPING SUBORDINATES WAITING

It is common to find executives who have few compunctions about keeping subordinates waiting. The cause of this tendency is not hard to isolate: the manager feels that because of his importance people won't mind waiting—they'll be so glad to see him.

The pastor of our church, Dr. Nathan Adams, gave his congregation this thought one day. "All my life I've been late," he said, "and recently the Lord has been showing me why.

It's arrogance—simple arrogance. I feel I'm important so the others should be happy I've come, even though late." He had made his point characteristically by using himself as an example. Doubtless many of his listeners identified with him.

An executive was taking one of his frequent tours through the plant with some visitors. He stopped for a short conversation with a lathe operator. After a few moments the executive became anxious about keeping the operator away from his work. On returning to his office with his visitors, he found two associates waiting to see him by previous appointment. He promised to be with them in a few minutes. Back in his office he explained to his visitors, "Don't worry about them —they can wait." He continued the visit for an additional 30 minutes while the associates waited.

Later the visitors learned that one of the associates was earning $18,000 a year and the other $30,000. The executive had not only kept them waiting for half an hour but had also disrupted their schedules and the supervision of their departments, causing an additional loss in management function. In recounting this incident Ross Barrett estimates that the straight time loss ran from $40 to $50. While the executive was very apologetic to his associates for keeping them waiting, he felt no real sense of loss in doing so. Yet while talking with the $3-an-hour lathe operator for five minutes (a $0.25 cost), he had felt a very keen sense of waste.[2]

This illustration depicts a lack of recognition of the true value of time. The "hurry up and wait" routine is especially irksome to effective subordinates. They are conscious of the time that is being wasted. They are quick to note the "urgency" with which some meetings are called and the insensitivity to the interruption in the schedules of all who are asked to attend. When this interruption is compounded by their being kept waiting, it is understandable that tempers rise and patience wanes.

If appointments were considered to be contracts between people, as Lawrence Appley suggests, there would be far more attention to promptness. A sign in my dentist's office reads, "Don't be late, you're hurting three—yourself, the next in line, and me."

INTERRUPTING SUBORDINATES' WORK

Managers with interruption-prone superiors will be allowed a chuckle as they are reminded of the boss who was constantly calling or dropping by to see "how the project is coming along that was being delayed by all the interruptions."

Many executives complain about the problem of keeping their subordinates "on the job." They speak with heartfelt conviction of the seemingly impossible task of insuring that subordinates give continuous concentration to the real objectives of the enterprise. The other side of this coin is the continual interruption they inflict on subordinates, diverting their efforts from these very objectives.

The boss who excuses his interruption with "This will only take you a couple of minutes, Bill" is oblivious to the substantial amount of time it will take Bill to get back on the track. Unfortunately Bill may not be well enough organized himself to realize what is happening to him.

Even meetings, as we saw in the last chapter, are not safe from such intrusions. All too often a conference with associates will be interrupted by a phone call or a drop-in visit from the boss asking "for a bit of information" or an answer to a routine query. A manager who is considerate of the time of subordinates takes measures to see that their time together is uninterrupted except for real emergencies.

One particularly important measure warrants reiterating: The boss should not allow his phone calls to subordinates to be "upgraded" by his secretary. It is not uncommon for the secretary, when her boss says he'd like to see one of his team, to place the call in a manner that implies "immediately." The recipient of the call has no alternative but to take it, whether he is the company president or a supervisor. A board chairman, for example, recounts what happened when he wanted to contact one of his division presidents. He asked his secretary to phone the president's office but neglected to tell her not to have him interrupted if he was busy. The president excused himself from a staff meeting to come to the phone, and was told by the board chairman only that he would be unable to meet with him at 3:00 that afternoon as they had planned.

In reflecting on this incident, the chairman said, "I know this happens a lot in my company. We're going to have to put a stop to it. It's a colossal waste of managerial time. Why should I be calling a president out of a meeting with his top staff just to tell him I can't meet with him?"

Helping Subordinates with Time

A colleague of mine observes that nothing tells subordinates so much about what's important to a manager as the way he spends his time. For example, a manager who is allowing interruptions to fragment his day is sending his subordinates the signal that the interruptions are more important to him than planning for and insuring the accomplishment of their objectives.

Subordinates should be encouraged to set time limits, eliminate unnecessary procedures, and streamline decision making. All these practices permit judgments to be made faster and mistakes to be discovered and corrected more quickly. Getting things done expeditiously gives everyone a sense of accomplishment and raises the level of morale in an organization. In an environment of rapidly accelerating change, speeding the tempo of decision making may be essential for survival.

TAKE A TIME LOG

The place to start with time management of subordinates is the time log described in Chapter 2. It is easy to visualize the reactions of subordinates to the suggestion that they take a time inventory. Many would view it as a threat or as a coercion. Others would see it as an imposition on an already overburdened schedule. Keeping a "laundry list" of everything one does every 15 minutes of the day for a week is not the most appealing proposal for a harried manager already frustrated by an inability to get all the things done he has to do in the limited time available. Top executives are themselves often reluctant to take the time inventory but urge their subordinates to do so. This reluctance is a direct reflection of the fallacy of omnipotence, which allows the top manager to believe that everyone else needs help but himself. Some feel on the contrary that they may indeed need help but do not wish to expose themselves. They are most likely to rationalize that they are too busy with more important things. The more appropriate view for the boss would be that he might learn something tremendously helpful to himself and that even if he didn't, by taking the inventory first, he has set the example and shown a willingness to participate in the use of a highly effective tool.

REQUIRE FOLLOWTHROUGH

Failure to follow through on assignments often entails repeated explanations and reminders to subordinates, obviously requiring effort and sizable chunks of time. The reasons for incomplete followthrough range from inadequate original instructions to an unrealistic schedule. Whatever the cause, the impact on managerial time utilization is serious. Frequently time losses result from the failure of subordinates to stay organized, to keep track of their assignments, to record progress made and responsibilities yet to be fulfilled, and perhaps most important of all, to maintain a clear, up-to-date list of their principal objectives and priorities.

A great benefit is derived by everyone concerned when a superior insists that his team follow assigned projects through. In so doing he is applying the rule of completed staff work. Derived from the military, the concept of completed staff work requires that the responsible subordinate review all facts germane to the situation, explore alternative approaches to accomplishing the mission, determine how to minimize any negative side effects, and select a course of action. If the superior is to make the final decision, all that is required is his approval, basically a yes-or-no decision. If the authority to decide rests with the subordinate, his boss need spend no time on the project at all. The gains in managerial effectiveness from adherence to the rule of completed staff work are multiple—not the least of which is that it discourages reverse delegation.

ENCOURAGE "MANAGING THE BOSS"

The subordinate who admits that he is distracted by interruptions—without naming the source—may need to be actively encouraged to "manage his boss." An effective technique that the boss might propose: the subordinate should have his own objectives and priorities clearly defined and constantly in front of him at all times so that when the boss drops in with "a couple of items to be handled," he can point out the effect this interruption will have on his top priority. This action assumes of course that the boss's request is not so trivial that it can be handled in a moment. In this manner the subordinate passes back to the boss, *where it belongs*, the decision of which priorities should be downgraded. Some alternatives could be offered, such as "How much of this do you need right away?" or "Will it be all right to postpone the deadline on the report to take care of these items?"

Five specific suggestions are pertinent to teaching subordinates the technique of "managing the boss":

1. Encourage them to question and to seek agreement on priorities rather than permitting their priorities to be destroyed without discussion. Be prepared to compromise if necessary to make the best use of both your times.

2. Ask them not to abuse your modified open door but to use it when they need it.

3. Counsel them neither to surrender to nor to rebel against boss-imposed time—but to anticipate it.

4. Advise them to be on guard against upgraded telephone messages, memos, and other calls on their time and to draw attention to examples. Special requests, especially from the head office, have a way of enlarging in urgency on their way down. As a result, managers often respond with far more time and effort than was originally envisioned or desired.

5. Make effective time management an organizationwide goal. Do not mandate changes without discussions and agreements. It is important that it be a team effort and that the decisions result from meaningful discussions.

What Does the Bottom Man Do?

In conferences with teams of administrators representing various levels of management, one question is very much in the wind during the discussion of delegation. What does the bottom man do? This plea comes from the man who has no one to whom to delegate. There is an answer, of course. If the managers at every level above him are inclined to work on less rather than more important things, the bottom man is likely to be trapped in trivia—the same sorts of time wasters that afflict the men on higher echelons. Should it not be possible for him to enhance his effectiveness as they do by setting objectives intelligently, assigning priorities to his tasks, managing by exception, and controlling by results?

Just as managers at other levels begin to get more done in less time with these practices, so the lower echelons in the organization should be able to use them to increase their productivity. In the end it ought to mean more production with fewer people.

A midwestern company has successfully implemented a program of replacing three clerical and supervisory people with two who have higher levels of capability. The larger salaries of the two more competent employees total less than the salaries for the three people who had originally been doing the work. The improved performance has demonstrated that with proper planning better results can be attained by fewer people.

The Team Concept

The "cascade" effect increases the consequences of ineffective time management on lower organizational levels in direct proportion to the increased numbers of managers at each level. A time waster with six subordinates will invariably cause problems for his entire team, which depends on him for instructions, approvals, information, motivation, clarification, and all the other vital links to the organization. Looking at it another way, one can see that a man will have difficulty maintaining his effective handling of time if his boss is ineffective as a time manager.

On the other hand, a manager acting solely in his own interests may make excellent use of his own time at the expense of colleagues, subordinates, and on rare occasions even his boss. One can visualize such a manager saying no to legitimate requests for assistance from peers. Not only are his practices detrimental to the overall effectiveness of the team, but in the end they almost surely will rebound on him when he finds himself in need of assistance from his associates. Anyone giving serious thought to time utilization in an organization will see the importance of viewing the problem from the perspective of the team rather than of the individual manager.

Another reason that the team concept of management is vital may be seen in the principle of dissipation of energy: time management appears to seek its lowest level. The poorest time user tends to drag others down to his level. If time management is viewed as a team rather than an individual endeavor, the force and effectiveness of the best time users can be strategically highlighted, protected by policy if necessary, and provided the support of top management, which may be essential for the notion to become pervasive.

Richard Nixon has long had an unusual policy with respect to the time of his team. When his secretary calls to ask for information or for a staff person to come to his office, she inquires whether the person has time. This courtesy provides his associate an opportunity to say that he is busy, identify his task, and request a delay. As evidence that this policy is no idle gesture, a White House assistant told me that as much as 50 percent of the time, staff members ask for delays to permit the completion of their immediate work.

This kind of deference in the interest of the team's time may come as a surprise in view of the demands on the time of the President of the United States. It is actually a highly skillful application of the cardinal rule of management—getting things done through others. In respecting the time of his team members, the boss is really respecting the importance of his own priorities. After all, if they are working on the things they ought to be, it will be *his* priorities they are accomplishing.

Chapter 9

Working with
Your Secretary

Of the many resources contributing to the manager's effectiveness, none is more critical than his secretary. Some managers act as though they want a secretary to mind her own business and simply do what she is told. The truth is that his business is also her business if he is to be as effective as he should.

As Cliff Bolerjack, president of Cimarron Equipment Corporation, puts it, "After gaining participation in and commitment to planning along with effective delegation of decision making, I place effective utilization of the secretary on the list of the executive's most important tasks. The time to be an effective manager is almost totally at her discretion." And Gerald Achenbach says, "There is nothing that can save time for a chief executive officer like a good secretary."

To test yourself on this "time saver," take the following quiz, designed by Ruth Gallinot, two-term president of the National Secretaries Association for Business Management.

Few secretaries would rate high on all counts or their titles should be changed to "office angel," but the implication is clear. Today's executive secretary must be knowledgeable and effective in the management of people as well as of paper and pushbuttons.

1. Does your secretary know the full range of your responsibilities and activities in your organization? Does she understand your personal goals and ambitions and how they fit in with corporate objectives?

2. Can you leave your office for as much as three or four weeks, confident that your business and personal affairs will be conducted responsibly and expeditiously in your absence?

3. Does she help you organize your time, coordinate your appointments and schedules, meet your deadlines—all without nagging and pestering you? Is she herself a well-organized person?

4. Does she initiate, handle and follow through on projects without your having to remind her about them?

5. Is she courteous, helpful, respectful and solicitous of your business associates, visitors, clients and customers? Do they speak of her favorably?

6. Is she imaginative? Creative? Does she present original ideas for your consideration? Does she suggest new ways to improve your work? Her work? Does she suggest new systems or procedures?

7. Is she resourceful? Does she show initiative in getting past a problem without running to you with her troubles?

8. Does she move paper efficiently? Can she tactfully pry loose papers and projects that have remained on your desk too long—and that other executives are waiting for? Does she shake loose data other executives are holding and that you are waiting for?

9. Are her basic secretarial skills (such as filing, stenography and telephone manner) beyond reproach?

10. Is she calm in a crisis? Gracious when tension mounts? When the pressure is on and you lose your temper or self-composure, does she shrug it off and continue to function as well as before?

11. Do you have her absolute loyalty and confidence? Can you trust her with confidential information, both personal and business?

12. Does she read widely and knowledgeably, bringing to your

attention published items pertinent to your business or personal affairs?

13. Is she a valuable source of corporate information, obtaining facts that would be difficult, awkward or impossible for you to obtain on your own?

14. Does she have a personal self-improvement program? Does she attend classes and lectures or participate in programs that are management-oriented? Does she try to learn more about your particular company, your particular job, your customers or your industry?

15. Is she articulate? Does she express herself well in summarizing information for you, both verbally and in writing? Does she give instructions clearly and precisely? Does she know how you feel about certain policies or practices, and does she communicate this to others as well as you do?

16. Does she work every day until her job is done, regardless of the hour? Does she willingly work nights or weekends when it is necessary?

17. Is she a manager in the sense that she can farm out her work to others when necessary? That is, can she delegate, supervise and take responsibility for work not completed by herself? Can she train or help train other members of your staff?

18. Can she handle routine matters and projects for you on a day-to-day basis without your intervention?

19. Does she keep track of vital dates for you, dates celebrated by your boss, family and customers (anniversaries, birthdays, religious holidays, vacations and such)?

20. Can she do basic research for you—gather information for a report, for example, or even write a rough first draft? [1]

How My Secretary Organized Me

I was fortunate in learning early about the importance of a competent secretary. When Shirley Wilson came to work for me, I was in difficulty, but I didn't know how much. Like many managers on the move, I was too busy climbing the executive ladder to recognize the extent of my plight.

Eager to demonstrate my capabilities, I continually involved myself in more and more projects, though each additional one meant less time to deal effectively with those I

already had. I scheduled appointments with less consideration of their real priority than of the importance of the people
to be seen. I made commitments without a realistic estimate
of the time required or the higher priorities that might inter-
vene. I delegated relatively few tasks and always with gnawing uncertainty, hoping they would not return to haunt me.

Under the illusion that loyalty should be as highly re-
warded as competence, I willingly worked long hours.
Neglecting my family, I practiced the art of getting more
things done rather than getting the few really important
things done well. Whenever feelings of insecurity arose, I
reassured myself with a look at my stacked desk. Anyone
with so many tasks to do must have a very important position! True, it was often difficult to find things on my desk, but
at least they were there. They could be located if necessary.
The more phone calls, the more people waiting to see me in
the morning, and the more interruptions, the surer I became
of my importance and the security of my position in the company.

No situation could have been more challenging for such an
able, competent secretary as Shirley Wilson. After a few
weeks she walked into my office one day and asked, "Mr.
Mackenzie, do you mind if I organize you?" Knowing that I
needed help, I accepted the offer without hesitation. Shirley,
however, had doubts about whether I really wanted to get organized, so she asked me how many times I had handled a
certain letter on top of one of the stacks on my desk. Thinking I would be on the safe side, I responded, "Oh, maybe 20
times."

We checked the date on the letter. It was three weeks old
—15 working days.

"How many times a day do you go through these stacks
looking for misplaced items?" she asked.

With a little less assurance, I answered, "It varies, I
suppose—perhaps 10 or 20."

"Perhaps 30 on a bad day?" she queried.

I assented and the mathematics became clear. Averaging

20 times a day over 15 days, it was possible that I had handled this letter in the vicinity of 300 times—not 20.

SEEING THE BOSS FIRST

Having proved her point, Shirley then described my office predicament from her point of view. As my secretary, she needed to see me early in the day for her "marching orders." Typically, however, when I arrived at 9:00 A.M., two or three people would be waiting to see me, often a phone call or two would need to be returned, and items of business hanging over from the previous day and week would be waiting to be cared for.

Always it seemed there were more important claims on my time than hers. She sometimes waited until well into the afternoon for the opportunity to see me for answers to her questions. She pointed to the frustration of always having the lowest priority, rarely being able to get fast answers when needed, and being ineffective while waiting for decisions or information she required before she could act. She suggested a reversal of priorities so that the first minutes of the morning would be available to her when she needed them.

This request led to a plan whereby my door would be closed for perhaps the first hour of the day. Shirley would sidetrack phoners and visitors, asking whether I might return the call or see the associate later. She would make appointments at the callers' wishes during my conference hours—we set these as 10:00 A.M. to 4:00 P.M. The first and last hours of the day would provide me uninterrupted time for concentration and allow her access to my office as needed for handling the increasing responsibilities she was gradually assuming. This plan insured that she could maintain cruising speed throughout the day.

SCREENING CALLS, VISITORS, AND MAIL

Once this policy was set, screening callers and visitors became relatively easy. The only exceptions permitted were emergencies. The hours from 10:00 to 4:00 proved more than adequate for team members who wished to see me. Shirley politely asked the purpose of each call to enable me to prepare for the visit. It also gave her an idea of how long the visit should take, and when in doubt she asked me. When the allotted time was up, she telephoned a reminder that time was passing and furnished a reason for terminating the meeting, saying something like "Don't forget your agenda for tomorrow" or perhaps "May I see you on something important in five minutes?" Whatever the question or comment, it enabled me to respond in a way that clearly indicated to the visitor that I had just a few minutes left. I could of course stand up and bring the appointment to a close.

In addition to screening calls and visits, Shirley screened mail. What could be handled by members of my team she sent to them, noting so to me when the matter was important enough for me to know about it. Routine complaints from customers were not included, but inquiries from a potentially large customer were.

I have found in the years since then that screening techniques are not found acceptable by all managers. Some simply don't believe in them either for visitors or for phone calls. Marketing-oriented executives frequently say, "Are you kidding? Let my secretary screen out the president of my largest account?" Other managers are not comfortable with screening even though they yearn for time to think without interruption. Still others fear that their secretary could not handle the job with the skill and tact required to avoid offending.

Top secretaries have gotten where they are by mastering these very skills of screening. Telephone companies provide professional coaching without charge in handling calls. Managers who fear losing a sale might consider whether the benefit of getting and staying organized perhaps outweighs that risk and whether the risk itself can be minimized by a better use of time; it's possible, for example, that the manager who takes all calls is letting his time be preempted by associates wanting to socialize just when big customers are trying to reach him. The effective secretary learns to recognize and to handle people quickly and well. She is cautious when she isn't sure.

William Lefsky reminds managers who take their own calls,

A secretary or assistant can field incoming calls more gracefully than you can. After all, when you say you're too busy to talk, the message will come as something of an affront, even if the caller is an old friend. When your assistant says you're too busy, the message is not so personal and can be taken more easily. . . .

The secretary answers the phone with, "Mr. Brown's office."

Then, when the caller asks for her boss, she answers, "I'm sorry, sir, but he's stepped away from his desk. May I have him call you back?" She writes down his name, company, and phone number—audibly saying, "Just to make sure I've got it right, is that Mr. Jones of the XYZ Corporation, phone 534-2933?" She can see her boss, seated at his desk, and she looks at him, arching her eyebrows questioningly.

If he nods *yes*, she says, "Please hold on a moment, Mr. Jones. I see him returning to his desk." If he shakes his head *no*, she says, "Thank you Mr. Jones. I'll see that he gets your message as soon as he returns." [2]

ATTACKING THE PAPER BLOCKADE

A Daniel Howard survey indicates that 69 percent of executives almost always reread letters before they are mailed.[3] As part of her attack on my stacked desk *and* my time wasting, Shirley not only assumed responsibility for the accuracy of all correspondence leaving the office but drafted replies to routine letters and answered local memos and letters by telephone. Her competent handling saved enormous managerial and secretarial time dictating, typing, mailing, and filing.

Then she tackled the problem of the paperwork I accumulated when traveling. She had observed the amount of time it took me on my return to sort through my briefcase, collect the various documents and the notes on decisions that had been made, and dictate appropriate letters concerning subjects that had grown a bit faint in my memory. She recommended the use of a portable dictating machine, which among its other uses would provide a convenient way to dictate letters on the plane immediately after visits, confirming actions taken while they were still fresh in mind. If the trip was to extend beyond a couple of days, Shirley would send me off with a self-addressed envelope, carrying air mail and special delivery postage, in which I would mail the dictation to her. By the time I returned from the trip, most of the letters would have been dispatched, since I delegated to Shirley the signing of the majority of my correspondence. She would hold for my personal signature only letters that were critical, sensitive, or legal in nature.

Having effectively imposed considerable order on my writing tasks, Shirley turned her organizing eye on my reading matter—more than 20 magazines that accumulated on my desk, including many that others had been inquiring about. She suggested that a routing list be attached to each periodical naming those who would be interested in seeing it. Two days would be allowed each manager to read it before passing it on to the next person. Readers would circle any article of interest in the table of contents and annotate it in the page margins, giving reasons for the article's importance and prospects for using ideas and initialing their markings. If any recipient was away from the office or unable to complete the reading in two days, his name would be moved to the bottom of the list. My name would be last, insuring that all those interested had seen the magazine before it came back to me. When it did, a quick glance would indicate whether the other readers had noted anything worthwhile. Magazines that consistently drew no comments were dropped from our subscription list.

This system of delegating reading kept magazines moving and insured that critical information was being picked up instead of hoarded on my desk where no one could get at it.

CREATING DESK-ORGANIZING FILES

At this point we could actually see the surface of my desk from time to time, and all that was needed to clear it was desk-organizing files. We began by setting up a system of working files, six folders headed "Urgent," "Dictate," "To Do," "Review," "File," and "Discard." It was Shirley's responsibility to see that all items coming into the office and not handled immediately were placed in the appropriate file.

"Urgent" matters were dealt with first, of course. Many days these were all I attended to; yet where else could my time have been spent more productively? The "To Do" file included all action items not falling under "Urgent" or "Dictate." The "Review" folder contained things that were of interest but not important. "File" meant simply for your information and then for filing as indicated. "Discard" was for materials not to be saved but of possible interest before being thrown away.

This system became indispensable in keeping my desk clear. It also facilitated rapid retrieval as well as convenient grouping of like tasks for much more efficient handling. Thus when I wanted to make calls, I would place a number of them, with all the data I needed appropriately backing up Shirley's notation on the purpose of the call.

Shirley next added a followup file to provide a place for holding items that needed future attention. While there are a variety of ways to set up a tickler file, I found Shirley's method very effective. This is the way it worked. When a memo or a letter came to my desk for which I did not yet have the required information or on which later action was needed, I would put a number in a circle in the upper right-hand corner indicating to Shirley how many days—say seven —before I would answer. She would immediately file this paper seven days ahead of the current date. When that day arrived she would pull it out, get the answer from me or whomever else I had indicated in a note, and handle the letter or memo accordingly. In the meantime it had been off my desk and in a place where either of us might have found it if necessary.

A tickler file is helpful when a secretary is sick and the boss or a replacement secretary has to start finding things. Insuring that items are catalogued so that they can be retrieved by anyone is a key to the entire filing system, as we saw in Chapter 4.

MONITORING PRIORITIES AND PROJECTS

A system of setting priorities a day ahead was quickly developed. By 4:00 in the afternoon, Shirley had placed on my desk her suggestions of the most important things to be accomplished the next day. She saw to it that when I arrived in the morning, my desk was cleared except for the most important project of the day. If the desk became cluttered during the day, she was authorized to clear it at any time unless I had placed a "Do not disturb" notation on an item. These understandings became useful aids in maintaining desk discipline and improving my concentration. I soon became aware of how easily I tended to stack up my desk unnecessarily, and eventually Shirley seldom needed to bail me out of my undesirable habit. Thus both of us could attend to the important work before us without delay or distraction.

We targeted certain things to be done by a certain date, and Shirley monitored progress on them. She checked on the progress far enough ahead of the deadline to assist me in getting to them in time to complete them on schedule. In some cases she took over something I was doing at the moment to free me for the No. 1 priority.

This monitoring of priorities, an extremely useful discipline, may be impossible if a secretary has more than one boss. The unity-of-command principle of management is violated more often in the case of the secretary than of any other position holder. Project management teams sometimes encounter difficulty in this regard, but authority conflicts are expected and therefore are more likely to be resolved. A secretary with more than one boss (some have three or four) finds that when the executives are not communicating among themselves about their expectations and requirements of her, very serious problems arise. The worst of these is that critical decisions concerning their relative priorities are left to her, placing on her the burden of trying to judge which tasks she should undertake first. The solution is for the bosses to communicate with each other in order to apportion priorities and to reach an understanding among themselves. Their decisions should then be communicated clearly to the secretary.

When Shirley had had some practice at monitoring my priorities, we developed a system for maintaining surveillance of projects of the men on my team. The first step was to prepare brief minutes for every meeting I conducted. They were limited when possible to a listing of the person who had the responsibility for carrying out the action, the decisions made, and the date due. These minutes became a useful tool for a followup procedure that Shirley recommended. She would keep the minutes at her desk and check periodically on all the items that had been decided upon. When action was completed she would mark the completion date. Items that were not completed were put first on the agenda of the next meeting under the heading "Unfinished Business." Managers knew they would be asked about the status of overdue projects at subsequent meetings. This reminder became a real incentive for them to complete their task on time.

Expanding this followup system, Shirley prepared an outline of all the important projects being worked on, grouping them under the men responsible for them and arranging them in order of either importance or deadline. They were listed in the left-hand column with three months of weekly columns following. Weekly reports of progress were expected on most projects scheduled for the next six months. Standard procedure when a new project was assigned was to schedule the frequency of progress reports. It was a simple matter for Shirley to check the dates on the progress control record and insure that the reports came in as planned. In reviewing them as they were submitted, she highlighted or annotated important points that in her opinion required urgent consideration. The responsible team members were encouraged to adopt a form of reporting by exception, to keep the amount of reading to a minimum. Thus a report on one project might read simply, "On target," whereas a project that was in difficulty would have to be explained. In the latter case, the report would identify the problem and indicate what was being done to correct it.

No other person had a more profound impact on my managerial effectiveness than Shirley Wilson. Like many people, I find it difficult to break bad habits and even more difficult to keep them broken. But the programs described above, even though they may not fit the particular style of every manager, were a great help to me.

Job Description for an Executive Secretary

Since his secretary is so critical to a manager's effectiveness, it is surprising to discover how rare good job descriptions are for this position. Practically all secretarial position descriptions include title, status, and reporting relationships. A few indicate the aims of the job in vague terms—such as "assisting the manager in achieving his objectives more effectively." The final and most important elements of the position, its responsibilities, are almost never outlined.

John Hamann, vice-president of Detroit Edison, and his secretary, Mrs. Clarice Lewis, have developed one of the best lists of responsibilities I have seen. With a few revisions, their specifications follow.

Mail. Answers are drafted to routine letters and submitted with current pertinent letters and file. Incoming mail is arranged in order of importance. Background material is gathered to facilitate the action indicated in the correspondence, and dates are checked regarding requests for future commitments. When the vice-president is absent for more than a few days, correspondence is acknowledged or referred to others for action.

Telephone. Telephone calls are handled promptly and with consideration and courtesy. Messages are recorded accurately, and passed on or referred to other departments along with any data necessary for action to be taken. Good judgment is exercised in giving out information to callers. When desirable, the secretary arranges to have the vice-president return the call at a set time and prepares a list of such grouped calls with relevant information (such as the purpose of the calls) and files for ready reference. All matters that can be handled elsewhere are referred diplomatically.

Appointments. Judgment is exercised in setting up appointments and meetings to consolidate free time. Information is obtained in advance as to the purpose, length of time required, and so forth. Material is organized for meetings, conference rooms are reserved, and notices are sent out in advance with the agenda. All appointments and meetings are recorded on calendars and updated daily.

Visitors. Concern for comfort and convenience is shown to all visitors. Reading matter and coffee are offered if waiting is necessary. Relevant files or data are on the vice-president's desk in time for his review before callers arrive. When visitors appear to be staying an unreasonable length of time, the secretary phones the vice-president to remind him of his next most urgent priority task and gives him a reason to terminate the conversation.

Human relations. The secretary cooperates with subordinates as well as with those in higher positions and shows a genuine interest in her job and the welfare of the company. Instructions are followed promptly and intelligently, and initiative is taken when appropriate. A dignified but friendly atmosphere is maintained in the office.

Office routines. A systematic followup procedure is maintained so that all reports, memoranda, and notices originating from the office are submitted on time. All telephone and mailing lists are kept up to date. Office supplies are ordered and housekeeping details arranged by planning ahead. "To be discussed with" lists are maintained for every person in regular contact and presented as reminders when needed.

Confidential matters. All gossip about the company and its employees is avoided, and personal matters are discreetly handled. Unless the secretary is otherwise instructed, she opens confidential mail but insures its confidential handling. Good judgment is shown in all conversations with visitors.

Travel arrangements. Transportation schedules are obtained well in advance of a trip, and a time and route schedule is submitted for approval. Transportation and hotel reservations are confirmed and financial arrangements completed. Business data, files, and supplies for the trip are assembled and three trip schedule cards are prepared, one for easy reference en route, one for family, and one for the office. These cards list hotels, flight numbers, telephone numbers, and names of contacts. An expense report is made out and submitted after the trip.

Filing. A classification system is developed to handle all material to be kept in office files and to facilitate immediate retrieval. A records retention plan is worked out and maintained to prevent unnecessary storage of files. Filing is kept up to date.

Objectives and priorities. Separate lists of long-range (over six months) and short-range objectives for the office are maintained. The secretary revises these monthly, indicating current status, and a regular rate of accomplishment is insured by systematic followup. Goals for the next day, and their relative priorities, are set and approved each day.

Job Description for a Boss

A very able and experienced secretary, Doris Nelson, says, "To me the three most important factors in the relationship between a boss and a secretary are consideration, confidence, and communication."

The boss can show consideration of the secretary in many ways: keeping organized so that necessary items can be located; being prepared for dictation to avoid delays, searches, and changes; advising the secretary where he is going and when he will return to aid her in handling inquiries during his absence; staying at his desk after placing a long-distance phone call; asking her for suggestions as to how he can help her be more effective.

Praise is a form of consideration. Too often secretaries hear only when things go wrong, not when they go right. Managers universally acknowledge that they are too skimping in their praise. We somehow simply do not make it a point to look for things on which to compliment our people. Secretaries, like all other key members of the team, are sensitive and appreciate acknowledgment and recognition when jobs are well done.

The executive demonstrates his confidence in his secretary by asking her opinion, suggesting that she write routine responses, and generally giving her a chance to show him what she can and would like to do. The boss also exhibits confidence in his secretary by supporting her if associates complain that she attempts to screen them. One top manager picked up his phone to hear such a complaint from a friend. In a loud voice that could be heard in the front office, he replied, "She said that? Well, I'll have to talk to her about that!" It would have been much better if he had said something like "Well, I'm sorry if she offended you. I'm sure she didn't mean to. I've asked her to request the caller's name and purpose so that she can give me any necessary information I may need for the call. This saves everyone's time, and in this way she can help both of us."

The subject of communication is a sensitive one for most secretaries simply because most bosses do not keep them adequately informed. Consequently they are unable to answer routine inquiries on such basic matters as where he is, when he will return, what he meant by a given memo, and so forth. These habits of course reflect on the secretary as much as on the boss. Keeping her informed makes her job much easier, results in a smoother-running organization, and puts her in a good light.

When I asked Mrs. Nelson to describe her "best boss," she wrote:

This gentleman kept me well informed on all details pertaining to office procedures and policy and let his people know what he expected of them and in turn what they could expect from him. He delegated responsibility and tasks equitably and backed his people. . . . His people always knew where they stood with him, an ideal for good working relationships. I was always allowed to run the front office and handle many routine matters that otherwise would have been very time-consuming for him.

Secretaries' most common suggestions for bosses include these:

1. Keep us informed (communicate). Tell us what you expect, how we're doing, what's behind the memo, why this is important, where you're going, and when you'll be back.

2. Let us make some decisions (confidence)—especially on routine matters when we *know* the answer—to gain confidence and to feel an important part of the team.

3. When you dictate, be prepared (consideration). Don't

fumble through papers, mumble into your fist, or change it all with an afterthought.

4. When you make appointments—keep them (consideration). Save us the embarrassment.

5. When others have requested information or decisions, get it back to them promptly (consideration).

6. Keep our work flowing (consideration).

Fundamental though this last point may seem, a competent secretary does not appreciate having her time idle. The executive is a poor manager if he fails to provide her with work. As one expert secretary puts it,

> Contrary to the comic strips on the subject, which usually aren't very funny, a secretary does not enjoy having plenty of free time to file her nails and read magazines. Sorry to say it, boss, but if you are not organized in your work, you limit my effectiveness. I enjoy the feeling which comes from doing a good job and accomplishing something. More than that, you can avoid that failing that some bosses have of thinking of lots of work to do just before quitting time.[4]

PROVIDE MANAGEMENT TRAINING

In the past, secretaries have been excluded from management training and development programs. Today companies are recognizing the importance of secretaries in the managerial function and are designing seminars for them. The chief executive of a Midwestern company observed, "It seems so elementary. With managerial effectiveness depending as much as it does upon the secretary, what's the sense in sending the manager and excluding the person who can make or break his effectiveness?"

Frequently, time management seminars for executives are followed by seminars for their secretaries in which a condensed version of the same principles is presented, tailored to the secretarial position. This practice provides an opportunity to inform each group of the expectations and helpful suggestions of the other.

The benefits of formal training in time management for secretaries accrue directly to their bosses, as the Midwestern manager implied. And, as Lawrence Appley put it: "One of the greatest difficulties of a president is the organization of his own time. If his secretary is as able as she should be, she will organize both him and his time and do it almost unnoticeably." [5]

Managers who do not have access to official training programs for their secretaries can develop the capabilities of these assistants by increasing their responsibilities on the job. Benjamin Cohn, of the Board of Cooperative Educational Services in New York, writes of an interesting experiment:

> After leaving a seminar around 3:30 P.M., I returned to my office, at which time my secretary brought in seven items for my consideration. I decided to see just how effective a secretary could be for a boss. After glancing at the items, I handed the folder back and asked her to handle them, advising me of her decisions before carrying them out. Her response was very positive. She seemed pleased and indicated that she didn't expect to have any problem with them.
>
> At about 4:30 P.M. she returned with three letters to be signed with regard to three of the cases. She told me how she planned to handle the other four. All seven were properly taken care of, requiring only about 15 minutes of my time instead of at least an hour that would normally have been required. Given the usual interruptions, it would have been well into the next day before I would have completed them. [6]

In seminars secretaries give evidence of insight into managerial problems that the managers themselves do not have. Proximity to the boss furnishes them opportunities for observation under many different circumstances. Who is in a better position to see the boss's impact on subordinates? Secretaries tend to be more sensitive to human feelings and often have a better sense of timing than their bosses. These associates merit and should be given responsibility and authority. A secretary who knows what the boss deems to be important and why is in a much better position to help him be effective.

PAY HER WHAT SHE'S WORTH

I am often asked the question, how much should a top secretary be paid? This question of course cannot be answered in general terms because situations vary so greatly. I suggest, however, that the manager begin by asking what he is worth to the company. Thomas Connellan, director of the Bureau of Industrial Relations, University of Michigan, observes that a good secretary doubles the effectiveness of the boss while a poor one can cut it in half. This is a fair beginning point for evaluating a secretary's worth.

Perhaps the underpayment of secretaries in the past has contributed to their underutilization. If his secretary's salary were comparable to that of the other members of the manager's team—and why shouldn't it be when she is the most critical factor in his effectiveness?—then he would be more likely to treat her as an important assistant. She would be included in executive staff meetings and management development programs and would represent the boss at appropriate functions just as would any other professional on the executive's team.

Because the secretary holds so critical a position, the manager simply must not accept less than the best. He should pay what it takes to get and keep the best. Her pay ought to be commensurate with that of his management team. Recognizing that length of service, job skills, and competence are valid criteria for compensation, test your thinking at this point. If you were advised that the secretary of a director of one of the highly sensitive government bureaus in Washington received a $25,000 annual salary, would your first thought be that it was the confidential nature of the job, her capabilities, or the length of service that accounts primarily for it? At the time of this writing, the secretary to the head of a major government agency is paid not $25,000 but $36,000, reportedly for all three reasons.

Perhaps the most explicit illustration of a secretary's value that I have ever heard is this account from Coleman Hogan, of the McCord Corporation: "The best thing that ever happened to me was having a secretary who wanted to work for a president. I was not the president, so she set out to help me make it. She had a tremendous impact on my effectiveness, and yes, I made it."

Appendix

How to Spring the Time Trap

Below are listed the time wasters I have most commonly encountered in eight years of consulting on time management with senior executives in a dozen countries.° To assist the reader in analyzing his own time wasters, possible causes and solutions are suggested for each. These are not intended to be exhaustive but merely to serve as guidelines for further diagnosis. Causes and solutions tend to be personal, while the time wasters themselves are universal in nature.

Time Waster	Possible Causes	Solutions
Lack of planning	Failure to see the benefit	Recognize that planning takes time but saves time in the end.
	Action orientation	Emphasize results, not activity.
	Success without it	Recognize that success is often in spite of, not because of, methods.
Lack of priorities	Lack of goals and objectives	Write down goals and objectives. Discuss priorities with subordinates.
Overcommitment	Broad interests	Say no.
	Confusion in priorities	Put first things first.

° The list is adapted from "Troubleshooting Chart for Time-Wasters," in R. Alec Mackenzie, *Managing Time at the Top* (New York: The Presidents Association, 1970).

Time Waster	*Possible Causes*	*Solutions*
	Failure to set priorities	Develop a personal philosophy of time. Relate priorities to a schedule of events.
Management by crisis	Lack of planning	Apply the same solutions as for lack of planning.
	Unrealistic time estimates	Allow more time. Allow for interruptions.
	Problem orientation	Be opportunity-oriented.
	Reluctance of subordinates to break bad news	Encourage fast transmission of information as essential for timely corrective action.
Haste	Impatience with detail	Take time to get it right. Save the time of doing it over.
	Responding to the urgent	Distinguish between the urgent and the important.
	Lack of planning ahead	Take time to plan. It repays itself many times over.
	Attempting too much in too little time	Attempt less. Delegate more.
Paperwork and reading	Knowledge explosion	Read selectively. Learn speed reading.
	Computeritis	Manage computer data by exception.
	Failure to screen	Remember the Pareto principle. Delegate reading to subordinates.

Time Waster	*Possible Causes*	*Solutions*
Routine and trivia	Lack of priorities	Set and concentrate on goals. Delegate nonessentials.
	Oversurveillance of subordinates	Delegate; then give subordinates their head. Look to results, not details or methods.
	Refusal to delegate; feeling of greater security dealing with operating detail	Recognize that without delegation it is impossible to get anything done through others.
Visitors	Enjoyment of socializing	Do it elsewhere. Meet visitors outside. Suggest lunch if necessary. Hold stand-up conferences.
	Inability to say no	Screen. Say no. Be unavailable. Modify the open-door policy.
Telephone	Lack of self-discipline	Screen and group calls. Be brief.
	Desire to be informed and involved	Stay uninvolved with all but essentials. Manage by exception.
Meetings	Fear of responsibility for decisions	Make decisions without meetings.
	Indecision	Make decisions even when some facts are missing.
	Overcommunication	Discourage unnecessary meetings. Convene only those needed.
	Poor leadership	Use agendas. Stick to the subject. Prepare concise minutes as soon as possible.

Time Waster	*Possible Causes*	*Solutions*
Indecision	Lack of confidence in the facts	Improve fact-finding and validating procedures.
	Insistence on all the facts—paralysis of analysis	Accept risks as inevitable. Decide without all facts.
	Fear of the consequences of a mistake	Delegate the right to be wrong. Use mistakes as a learning process.
	Lack of a rational decision-making process	Get facts, set goals, investigate alternatives and negative consequences, make the decision, and implement it.
Lack of delegation	Fear of subordinates' inadequacy	Train. Allow mistakes. Replace if necessary.
	Fear of subordinates' competence	Delegate fully. Give credit. Insure corporate growth to maintain challenge.
	Work overload on subordinates	Balance the workload. Staff up. Reorder priorities.

Notes

CHAPTER 1

1. Quoted in Ted W. Engstrom and R. Alec Mackenzie, *Managing Your Time* (Grand Rapids, Mich.: Zondervan, 1967).
2. Peter F. Drucker, "How to Be an Effective Executive," *Nation's Business*, April 1961.
3. Yair Aharoni, "The Foreign Investment Decision Process" (Boston: Harvard Business School, Division of Research, 1966).
4. John Kitching, "Why Do Mergers Miscarry?", *Harvard Business Review*, November–December 1967.
5. Curtis H. Jones, "The Money Value of Time," *Harvard Business Review*, July–August 1968.
6. "Management Outlook," *Business Week*, March 14, 1970.
7. Answers: A—German managers; B—college presidents; C—Canadian military officers; D—black leaders of religious organizations.
8. Quoted in "Executive Workloads—The Triumph of Trivia," *The Wall Street Journal*, August 13, 1968.
9. Herman C. Krannert, "The Time Wasters," *The Forum*, Spring 1969.
10. Wayne E. Oates, *Confessions of a Workaholic* (New York: World, 1971).
11. Clarence B. Randall, *The Folklore of Management* (Boston: Little, Brown, 1961).
12. Ibid.
13. Charles H. Ford, "How to Pep Up a Sluggish Company," *Business Management*, August 1968.
14. Joseph M. Trickett, "A More Effective Use of Time," *California Management Review*, Summer 1962.
15. Caroline Bird and Thomas D. Yutzy, "The Tyranny of Time: Results Achieved Versus Hours Spent," *Management Review*, August 1965.
16. Dorothy L. Sayers, *Creed or Chaos?* (London: Methuen, 1954).

CHAPTER 2

1. See Charles D. Flory and R. Alec Mackenzie, *The Credibility Gap in Management* (New York: Van Nostrand Reinhold, 1971).

2. Walter H. Judd, "Critique on Conflict," *Collegiate Challenge*, Vol. 5, No. 1, January 1966.

3. Robert F. Pearse, "The Effects of an Executive's Leadership Style on His Time Management Practices" (Boston: mimeo., 1972).

4. Glenn A. Bassett, "The Qualifications of the Manager," *California Management Review*, Winter 1969.

5. Sune Carlson, *Executive Behavior: A Study of the Work Load and the Working Methods of Managing Directors* (Stockholm: Stromberg, 1951).

6. Ibid.

7. William James, "Making Habits Work for You," *Reader's Digest*, August 1967.

8. Karl Menninger, introduction to James, op. cit.

9. James, op. cit.

10. Auren Uris, *The Executive Deskbook* (New York: Van Nostrand Reinhold, 1970).

11. "Bits and Pieces," *The Economic Press*, March 1969.

12. Norman Vincent Peale, "You Can Stop Being a Procrastinator," *Reader's Digest*, January 1972.

13. John F. Mee, "The Zeigarnik Effect," *Business Horizons*, June 1969.

14. Orison Swett Marden, *Do It to a Finish* (New York: Crowell, 1909).

15. Louis A. Allen, *The Management Profession* (New York: McGraw-Hill, 1964).

CHAPTER 3

1. Quoted in Ted W. Engstrom and R. Alec Mackenzie, *Managing Your Time* (Grand Rapids, Mich.: Zondervan, 1967).

2. Recounted in Donald V. Schoeller, "How to Find an Extra Golden Hour Each Day" (Norwalk, Conn.: monograph).

3. Quoted in R. Alec Mackenzie, *Managing Time at the Top* (New York: The Presidents Association, 1970).

4. Charles E. Hummel, *The Tyranny of the Urgent* (Chicago: Inter-Varsity, 1967).

5. Ralph J. Cordiner, cited in *The Work of a Professional Manager*, Book III of *Professional Management in General Electric* (New York: General Electric Company, 1954).

6. Leo B. Moore, "Managerial Time," *Industrial Management Review*, Spring 1968.

7. "Indochina: Tough Days on the Trail," *Time*, March 8, 1971.

8. J. Roger Morrison, "Britain's Quiet Managerial Revolution," *Management Today*, November 1967.

9. "People at Work: The Chief Executive's Time," *Personnel,* May–June 1968.

10. Quoted in Joseph D. Cooper, *How to Get More Done in Less Time* (Garden City, N.Y.: Doubleday, 1962).

11. Ross A. Webber, *Time and Management* (New York: Van Nostrand Reinhold, 1972).

12. Auren Uris, *The Efficient Executive* (New York: McGraw-Hill, 1957).

13. F. D. Barrett, "The Management of Time," *The Business Quarterly* (Western Ontario School of Business), Spring 1969.

14. Dean Acheson, "Thoughts About Thoughts in High Places," *The New York Times Magazine,* October 11, 1959.

15. W. Dickerson Hogue, "What Does Priority Mean?", *Business Horizons,* December 1970.

16. Joseph M. Juran, *Managerial Breakthrough* (New York: McGraw-Hill, 1964).

17. Auren Uris, *The Executive Deskbook* (New York: Van Nostrand Reinhold, 1970).

18. Lester R. Bittel, *Management by Exception* (New York: McGraw-Hill, 1964).

19. Quoted in Chaplin Tyler, "Steps in Becoming a Better Manager," *Chemical Engineering,* April 30, 1962.

20. Herman C. Krannert, "The Time Wasters," *The Forum,* Spring 1969.

21. Frank A. Nunlist, "Wanted: Executive Time Power," *Dun's Review,* October 1967.

22. Curtis W. Symonds, *A Design for Business Intelligence* (AMA, 1971).

23. Theodore Levitt, *The Marketing Mode* (New York: McGraw-Hill, 1969).

24. Robert R. Updegraff, *All the Time You Need* (Englewood Cliffs, N.J.: Prentice-Hall, 1958).

25. E. B. Osborn, *Executive Development Manual* (New York: Economics Laboratory, Inc., September 1959). Copyright © 1959 by Economics Laboratory, Inc. Reprinted by permission.

CHAPTER 4

1. E. B. Osborn, *Executive Development Manual* (New York: Economics Laboratory, Inc., September 1959).

2. Sune Carlson, *Executive Behavior: A Study of the Work Load and the Working Methods of Managing Directors* (Stockholm: Stromberg, 1951).

3. Auren Uris, *The Executive Deskbook* (New York: Van Nostrand Reinhold, 1970).

4. *Time,* March 28, 1969.

5. "Executive Workloads—The Triumph of Trivia," *The Wall Street Journal*, August 13, 1968.

6. Eric Webster, "Memo Mania," *Management Review*, September 1967.

7. "People at Work: The Chief Executive's Time," *Personnel*, May–June 1968.

8. Gerard P. O'Shea, *The New Reading* (New York: Oxbridge Publishing Co., 1972).

9. Both the reading test and the questions that follow it are taken from Carl Heyel, *Organizing Your Job in Management* (AMA, 1960).

10. Answers: 1—T; 2—F; 3—T; 4—T; 5—F; 6—T; 7—T; 8—F; 9—F; 10—T.

11. David B. Orr and Herbert L. Friedman, "Effects of Massed Practice on Comprehension of Time-compressed Speech," *Journal of Educational Psychology*, Vol. LIX, No. 1, 1968.

12. James McCay, *The Management of Time* (Englewood Cliffs, N.J.: Prentice-Hall, 1959).

CHAPTER 5

1. George J. Berkwitt, "The Case of the Fragmented Manager," *Dun's Review*, April 1969.

2. Sune Carlson, *Executive Behavior: A Study of the Work Load and the Working Methods of Managing Directors* (Stockholm: Stromberg, 1951).

3. Curtis W. Symonds, *A Design for Business Intelligence* (AMA, 1971).

4. Don Mitchell, *Top Man: Reflections of a Chief Executive* (AMA, 1970).

5. Joseph M. Trickett, "A More Effective Use of Time," *California Management Review*, Summer 1962.

6. Quoted from an advertisement in *Forbes*, November 15, 1970.

7. Quoted in "Jesters to the Court of Business," *Business Week*, September 5, 1971.

8. Quoted in Russell L. Packard, "For Those Who Must Lead," *The Hillsdale College Leadership Letter*, January 1968.

9. Hensleigh C. Wedgwood, "Fewer Camels, More Horses," *Personnel*, July–August 1967.

10. Ira S. Gottfried, "Effective Use of Executive Time," *Data Processing: Proceedings of the 1969 Data Processing Conference* (Park Ridge, Ill.: Data Processing Management Association, 1969).

11. Wedgwood, op. cit.

12. Antony Jay, *Corporation Man* (New York: Random House, 1971).

13. *The New York Times*, January 4, 1972.

CHAPTER 6

1. Auren, Uris, *The Executive Desk Book* (New York: Van Nostrand Reinhold, 1970).
2. Quoted in Donald A. Laird and Eleanor C. Laird, *The Technique of Getting Things Done* (New York: McGraw-Hill, 1947).
3. Edward C. Bursk and Charles H. Ford, "Organizing for Faster Decisions," *Management Review*, April 1971.
4. Quoted in *Nation's Business*, April 1956.
5. Charles H. Ford, "Decisions," *TWA Ambassador*, December 1970.
6. David A. Emery, "Managerial Leadership Through Motivation by Objectives," address to the American Psychological Association, September 1968.
7. Saul W. Gellerman, "Management Outlook," *Business Week*, July 13, 1968.
8. Charles H. Ford, "How to Pep Up a Sluggish Company," *Business Management*, August 1968.
9. Ibid.

CHAPTER 7

1. William H. Newman, Charles E. Summer, and E. Kirby Warren, *The Process of Management* (Englewood Cliffs, N.J.: Prentice-Hall, 1967).
2. Laurence J. Peter and Raymond Hull, *The Peter Principle* (New York: Morrow, 1969).
3. Ibid.
4. Raymond O. Loen, "Manager or Doer: A Test for Top Executives," *Business Management*, May 1966.
5. Ibid. Copyright © 1966 by CCM Professional Magazines, Inc. All rights reserved. This quiz and the answers following it are reprinted by permission.
6. Ibid.
7. See R. Alec Mackenzie, "The Management Process in 3D," *Harvard Business Review*, November–December 1969.
8. Louis A. Allen, *The Management Profession* (New York: McGraw-Hill, 1964).
9. Reported in Robert Smith, "Time" (tape recording; Des Plaines, Ill.: Tape Cassette Recording).
10. William H. Newman, "Overcoming Obstacles to Effective Delegation," *Management Review*, January 1956.
11. Auren Uris, *The Executive Deskbook* (New York: Van Nostrand Reinhold, 1970).
12. David Brown, "Why Delegation Works—and Why It Doesn't," *Personnel*, January–February 1967.
13. Newman, op. cit.

14. "Man in Business," *The New York Times,* December 6, 1970.

CHAPTER 8

1. Ross Barrett, *Executive Time Control Program* (Englewood Cliffs, N.J.: Prentice-Hall, 1964).
2. Ibid.

CHAPTER 9

1. Ruth Gallinot, "How Good Is Your Personal Secretary?" *Business Management,* October 1965. Copyright © 1965 by CCM Professional Magazines, Inc. All rights reserved. Reprinted by permission.
2. William Lefsky, "Are Your Phone Calls Being Screened Tactfully?" *Supervisory Management,* December 1969.
3. "Executive Workloads—The Triumph of Trivia," *The Wall Street Journal,* August 13, 1968.
4. Laurence J. Taylor, "Secretary—Take a Memo?", *The Hillsdale College Leadership Letter,* February 1965.
5. Lawrence A. Appley, "Miss Assistant President," *Management News,* November 1962.
6. Personal letter from Benjamin Cohn.

Index